HORSE
BY
HORSE

HORSE BY HORSE

WINDWARD

A QED BOOK
Windward
An imprint owned by
W.H. Smith & Son Ltd.
Registered No 237811 England

Trading as WHS Distributors Euston Street,
Freemen's Common, Aylestone Road,
Leicester LE2 7SS
ISBN 0 7112 0016 5

Filmset in Britain by Abettatype Ltd.
Colour origination in Italy by Starf Photolito
SRL, Rome
Printed in Italy by New Interlitho SPA, Milan.

This book is based on some of the material
from The Complete Book of the Horse. It was
designed and produced by QED Publishing
Limited, 32 Kingly Court, London W1
Editorial Director Jeremy Harwood
Art Director Alastair Campbell
Production Director Edward Kinsey
Art Editor David Mallott
Art and editorial co-ordination Heather Jackson
Illustrators Kai Choi, Harry Clow,
Christopher Forsey, Tony Graham, Rory
Kee, Elaine Keenan, Edwina Keene, Abdul
Aziz Khan, Kathleen McDougall, Martin
Woodford, Kathy Wyatt, David Staples,
Jim Marks.
Technical Consultants
Pamela MacGregor-Morris, Jane Kidd.

Contents

Introduction

Throughout history, the horse has been one of the closest animals to man; today, with the great interest in horses shown by people of all ages, the bond is becoming ever closer.

The structure of the book

This book is designed to answer some of the basic questions such people ask about the horse: where did it originate and how did it evolve into the animal we know today? How is it physically made? What are the characteristics of the many breeds of horse in the world and how do they differ in character as well as appearance? The chapter on Evolution takes the story of the horse from the emergence of the so-called 'dawn horse' over 55 million years of geological time until the evolution of *Equus*. The Points of the Horse chapter examines the animal's physical make-up, while the section on the Breeds of the World covers the horses concerned according to geographic area and then proceeds to detailed examination of individual breeds through illustration and extensive captions. For ease of reference, the bulk of this section is in alphabetical order.

A good horse

What makes a good horse is a question debated by riders all over the world and it is one to which there is no single answer. There is no doubt, however, that correct breeding is one of the most important factors. This is a complex business and should never be undertaken lightly; at the very top of the scale, breeding is a multi-million dollar and pound industry, while, even at the domestic level, it can still be an extremely expensive undertaking. Firstly, it is vital that both parents are of as sound a stock as possible, though, in some cases, the virtues of a stallion can be used to correct some of the faults of the mare.

The stages of pregnancy

Having decided to breed, the next step is to choose a suitable stud. Mares come into season at regular intervals between eighteen and twenty-one days; it is at this time that they can be 'served' (inseminated) by a stallion. After this has taken place, most studs keep the mare for about six weeks to ensure as far as possible that the animal concerned has 'held' to the service. This is checked again through veterinary examination of blood and urine samples at a later date. Before the mare is even accepted by the stud, a veterinary certificate is usually required, guaranteeing that the animal is free from disease and infection.

Mating itself takes only a couple of minutes, but the preparations can last for much longer. At many studs a lower-grade stallion called a 'teaser' is kept to try mares in order to establish whether they are ready for service. During the actual process itself, both mare and stallion are kept firmly under control by stud grooms. To aid in this, both are bridled throughout.

Pregnancy lasts for approximately eleven months. During this time, the mare needs little extra care, apart from a slightly richer diet. Provided that she is not over-exerted, she can be safely ridden to an advanced stage of pregnancy — to a maximum of seven months — as exercise is good for all pregnant animals.

Ponies are often thought to foal best in the field, as they do in the wild; the more well-bred the breed, however, the more attention that will be necessary. Again, the best thing to do is to book the mare into a stud well in advance of the expected birth date. There, she will receive expert care and constant supervision — many of the best studs, for instance, now have closed-circuit television to help in this task.

Birth and after

The first signs of labour are when the mare begins to pace around restlessly, swishing her tail and glancing at her sides. Wax forms on the udder and drops off the teats. As the labour pains intensify, the mare lies down. Birth is imminent when she releases her waters — that is, when the membranes of the sack containing the foal and its protective fluid break.

Delivery itself usually presents few problems, unless the foal is abnormally presented. This can occur if, say, the hind end is presented foremost — what is known as a breech presentation. In most cases, manipulation is the answer and this is why it is always preferable to have an expert on call. Again taking the example of breech presentation, it is essential to make sure that both the hind legs are in the birth passage. This must be done quickly, as otherwise the umbilical cord supplying air to the foal can become trapped. If this happens, the foal will drown in the fluid contained in the protective membrane.

When birth has been completed, the mare recovers swiftly in almost all cases. So, too, does the foal; after an initial licking by its mother, it will stand and start to suckle from her teats. This first suck is all important, as the milk contains vitamin-rich colostrum, which gives the foal natural imunity against several juvenile diseases. It also stimulates the bowels into action.

Provided no problems have arisen, mare and foal can both be turned out for exercise a day after the birth. A couple of days after that, the first steps in the foal's training can begin, when a small head collar, known as a slip, is put on the animal. This enables the owner to accustom the foal to being led and handled — the latter is essential if, say, injections are necessary. Slowly, too, it can be given solid food

Life progresses in a regular routine until the foal is ready to be weaned. The best way to do this is to separate it from its mother and keep it in a loose box for two weeks. Solid food should by now be readily accepted; milk pellets can be added if the animal appears to be loosing condition. After this, the foal has to get used to a new routine of field by day and loose box by night. It helps if a companion can be provided as a substitute for the mother — another foal is best — but it is also important to keep the two animals separate at feeding times.

This pattern of life continues for a year or so — the time spent outdoors increasing as the foal gets tougher — until the time comes for it to be broken. The only additional precaution necessary is a regular check on the feet in case of disease.

7

The Evolution of the Horse

The horse as we know it today is the product of a long evolutionary chain stretching back for literally thousands of years. Before the end of the Ice Age, some 12,000 to 15,000 years ago, the ancestors of present-day *Equus Caballos* roamed the world's grassy plains. These, in turn, emerged as a result of a process spanning some 55 million years of geological time.

The 'dawn horse'

The first of these ancestors was *Eohippus* or *Hyracotherium* (the latter is the accepted scientific name), which flourished from some 55 to 38 million years ago and is considered the first distinct horse. This breed was small in stature — about the size of a fox terrier — but was a notable advance over its own *condylarth* ancestors. The chief difference was the number of digits in each foot — *Hyracotherium* had four on the fore feet and three on the hind, as opposed to the five of the *condylarths*. Its legs were also longer, while the animal's teeth, jaws and skull were deeper and longer than those of its predecessors, making it more suited to grazing. Longer limbs, for their part, meant that *Hyracotherium's* pace was increased, an especially important factor in its battle for survival against its various predator enemies. In addition, recent research has shown that the brain of *Hyracotherium* and other early horses were progressive in their evolution, when compared with other primitive mammals, such as their *condylarth* relatives.

Hyracotherium was also geographically widespread; traces of it have been found in both the New and the Old Worlds.

From four toes to three

About 38 million years ago, the first three-toed horses emerged, developing from one strain of *Hyracotherium* as the others died out. There were two groups of these — primitive browsers, feeding on leafy vegetation, and advanced grazers, feeding on grass. The browsers emerged first — they became extinct about 11 million years ago — to be followed later by the grazers.

Both groups were bigger than *Hyra-*

8

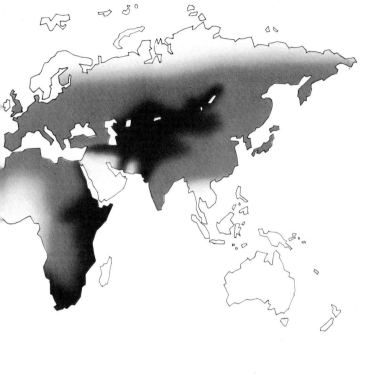

How Equus was distributed during the Pleistocene Epoch and where it is found in the wild today. Equus originated some 3-4 million years ago and spread from its North American homeland to many parts of the world. At the end of the last Ice Age, however, many varieties became extinct, possibly because of climatic change. The distribution of wild Equus today is relatively limited.

:otherium; both had longer legs; and both had even more effective means of eating. Like *Hyracotherium,* too, they spread widely, starting in North America to reach the Old World some 20 million years ago. Yet, it was the development of the grazers as an independent entity that made this period an especially important one in horse history, for the change represented an important diversification of feeding habits in the evolutionary process. Specialized grazing meant that teeth, skull and jaws had to adapt to cope with the increased wear and tear of chewing abrasive grasses; accordingly all of them became deeper as

time went by.

The main home of these grazers was in North America, though one group — the *Hipparions* — successfully migrated from the New World to the Old some 10 to 11 million years ago. It was on the grassy plains of North America, too, that the first one-toes horses emerged around 15 million years ago.

The emergence of Equus

The first one-toed horses were grazers, like their three-toed ancestors, though they apparently emerged from only one type in North America. This transition from three

9

toes to one was a natural evolutionary consequence, as the size of the side digits gradually became smaller until only the central one played any part in running. On the whole, these horses were bigger bodied than their predecessors, while their molars, skull and jaws were also enlarged.

Most of these one-toed horses were located in Central and North America and it was in the American north that the first representatives of *Equus* developed. These were descended from the one-toed *Dinohippus* and emerged between three and four million years ago. They spread quickly, becoming the most geographically diverse of of all ancestral horses; North, Central and South America, Asia, Europe and Africa all had their colonies. They also consisted of many different species, though, in common with many other large mammals, most of these became extinct by the end of the last Ice Age, about 12,000 to 15,000 years ago.

The reasons for this sudden drastic decline are obscure. Some experts think it was due to the change in climate or the influence of man, while others suggest a combination of these or still more factors. Whatever the cause, the process was severe — particularly in America, the ancestral home of *Equus*. There, horses totally vanished from the scene; they were not to reappear until the Spanish *conquistadores* landed in Mexico in the early 16th century AD.

From the wild to domestication
By the end of this period, *Equus* had reached a recognisably modern form. During this long evolutionary progress, several trends had become apparent — all a direct result of the constant battle for survival in a sometimes hostile environ-

ment. On the whole, horses gradually increased in size, though there were times when some remained the same size or even grew smaller. Changes in skull and limbs also took place, as horses adapted to better suit themselves for grazing and running.

The next major step was the work of an external force — that of man. In around 3000 BC, probably in Asiatic Russia, the horse was first domesticated. The only major area of controversy here is whether a single type of horse was involved or whether several types were domesticated at the same time. Some experts believe that two distinct kinds — the now extinct tarpan and Przewalski's horse were involved — but others argue that the one is related to the other.

In any event, what is certain is that, from there, the knowledge of domestication spread rapidly and widely;

The source of knowledge
The evolution of the horse is a fascinating and complex subject that today attracts scientists all over the world. The major source of knowledge is based on the rich fossil deposits of western North America — though the first description of *Hydracotherium* was in fact based on the finds made in the marshes around London in 1839. The discovery, made by the British paleontologist Sir Richard Owen, did much to inspire the work of successors in the field, particularly in the USA.

Chief amongst these scientists was O.C Marsh, the Professor of Paleontology at Yale University in the Mid-nineteenth century. It was Marsh who discovered *Eohippus* — the 'dawn horse' — the oldest horse in North America. And it was on his work that others built to create much of the knowledge that we possess today.

The family tree of the horse, showing the animal's evolutionary development since the emergence of Hyracotherium, the ancestral four-toed horse, in the Eocene Epoch some 55 million years ago. As the diagram shows, the evolutionary path was by no means straightforward; during the Miocene Epoch in particular, there were many divergences from it.

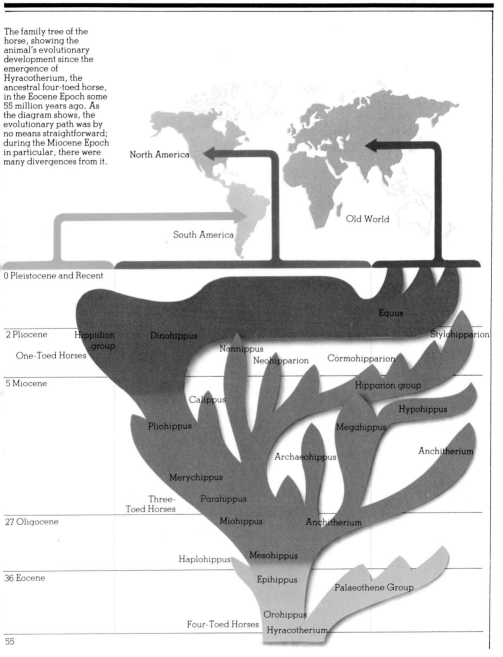

North America

Old World

South America

0 Pleistocene and Recent

Equus

2 Pliocene — Hippidion group — Dinohippus — Stylohipparion

One-Toed Horses — Nannippus

Neohipparion — Cormohipparion

5 Miocene

Calippus — Hipparion group

Hypohippus

Pliohippus — Megahippus

Archaeohippus — Anchitherium

Merychippus

Three-Toed Horses — Parahippus

27 Oligocene — Miohippus — Anchitherium

Haplohippus — Mesohippus

36 Eocene — Epihippus

Palaeothene Group

Orohippus

Four-Toed Horses — Hyracotherium

55

The Points of the Horse

Some of the common body colours of the horse. The commonest are bay, chestnut, black and brown, though there are many possible varieties within these broad definitions. Thoroughbreds can be bay/brown, grey and roan, for instance; non-Thoroughbreds can be dun, cream, piebald, odd-coloured, palomino, skewbald and so on. In doubtful cases, colouring is officially defined according to that of the points — the muzzle, tip of the ears, mane, tail and lower legs.

What is most surprising about the horse is that, physically, it is not ideally suited to many of the tasks it is asked to perform by man. Thus, all riders — whether beginners or experts — cannot be considered complete authorities unless they possess at least a basic knowledge of the physical make-up of the animal they ride.

Such knowledge is essential; at a sale, for instance, the awareness that a good riding horse should have plenty of heart room to give it stamina and toughness may save a buyer from an expensive mistake. On a day-to-day basis, too, knowledge of the so-called points of the horse helps to lessen the risk of injury, particularly where the sensitive joints and muscles are concerned. Such factors should always be born in mind by a rider in his or her approach to the horse and what he or she expects it to do.

The feet

Of all the points of the horse, feet, followed by limbs, come foremost in order of importance; both in the domestic state and in the wild they are the key to the animal's survival. They therefore need to be as correctly conformed as possible — in other words, as perfect as nature will allow.

Well-formed feet are vital, as these have to carry weight and absorb the shock of movement; when a horse jumps, for example, the entire weight of animal and rider falls on one forefoot at the moment of landing. The delicate interior is protected

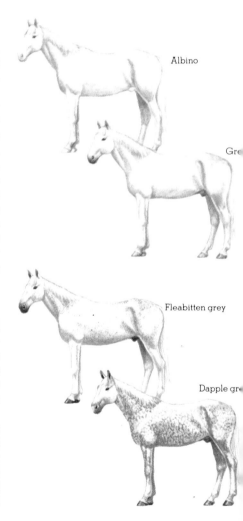

Albino

Gre

Fleabitten grey

Dapple gr

Chestnut

Odd-coloured

Liver chestnut

Strawberry roan

Black

Blue roan

Piebald

Palomino

Skewbald

Bay

Yellow dun

Brown

13

by an outer layer of hoof. This grows at a rate of about 5 mm (0.2 in) per month, so that wear and tear is constantly repaired. Within the foot are the navicular and pedal bones — the end of the pedal being attached to the digital flexor tendon — the digital pad, part of the second phalanx, the corono-pedal joint, cartilages, blood vessels and nerves. The most important of these are the sensitive laminae, which carry food to the hoof and also link it with the bones.

The hoof itself consists of walls, bars, sole and frog. It is particularly important that the frog is sound and well-developed; it acts as an anti-slip device and helps to absorb concussion.

The hindlegs

The hindlegs are the power house of the horse and so are one of its most important features. They are linked to the body by the stifle joint, which, with its patella, functions in a similar manner to the human knee and knee cap. Acting like a pulley block, the patella strengthens the muscles extending the stifle. This, in turn, is controlled by the same ligaments and muscles as the hock, so that the two are synchronized in their movements.

Proceeding down the leg, there follows the gaskin, or second thigh, which runs into the hock. Consisting of a series of joints tightly bound together by ligaments, this is probably the most important part of the leg as it is the main propulsive agent. It articulates directly with the tibia through a single bone — the astralagus.

A good hock is large, flat and almost square when viewed from the side: it is a sign of weakness if the feature looks turned inwards when viewed from the back; the opposite, however, is a sign of strength.

The point of the hock, too, should be well defined, or the strain on the curb ligament will be intensified. Tendons should also stand out clearly, while the lower leg should not thicken.

A further feature to look for is short cannon bones; running from fetlock to hock and fetlock to knee, these are another sign of strength. The fetlock joint itself should be well-defined and not swollen. This leads on to the pastern. This should be fairly short and should slope at a gentle angle. The more acute the angle, the greater the strain put upon the suspensory tendons and ligaments. However, if the pastern is too short and upright, it cannot fulfill its job of absorbing concussion. The effects of this are then passed directly to the joints — another bad fault.

The foreleg

As the horse has no equivalent to the human collar bone, the foreleg is linked to the main part of the body solely by muscle and ligamentous tissue. Though this arrangement ensures that a great deal of concussion is absorbed, rather than being passed on to the spine, it also means that the muscles can easily be strained if undue pressure is placed upon them. As a consequence, it is particularly important to treat all suspected strains promptly.

The foreleg extends from the body below the point of the shoulder. The forearm runs down into the knee; the former should be strong, as a weak forearm means lack of muscle. Like the hock, the knee should be broad, flat and prominent to take the weight of the body. The cannon, with clearly-visible tendons, runs down into the fetlock, which is separated from the foot by the pastern.

From the front, cannon and forearm

Facial markings are important means of individual identification. Here, some of the common ones are shown. In the case of a star, the position, as well as size and shape, should be noted; a stripe should be classed as either narrow or broad. A star followed by a stripe is called a disjointed blaze.

White face

Stripe

Blaze

Snip

Star

White leg markings are also important in identification and should be listed accordingly in, say, a breeding certificate. So, too, should variations in hoof colour. The term stocking (second illustration) is commonly used to describe a patch of white extending over the fetlock; a sock (third illustration) stretches to knee or hock. Other such marks are defined according to their site.

15

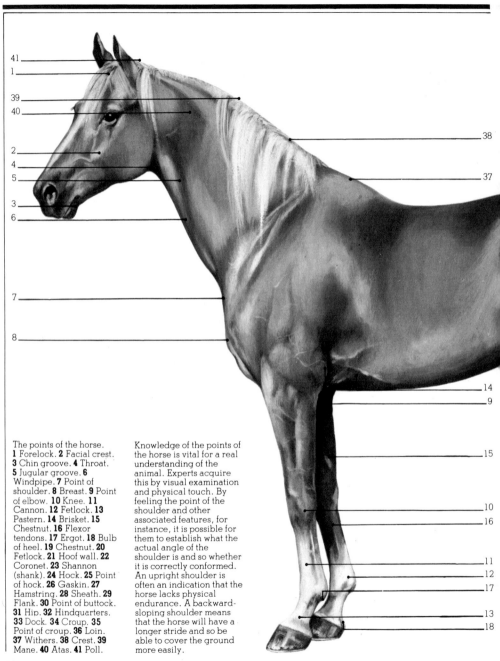

The points of the horse. 1 Forelock. 2 Facial crest. 3 Chin groove. 4 Throat. 5 Jugular groove. 6 Windpipe. 7 Point of shoulder. 8 Breast. 9 Point of elbow. 10 Knee. 11 Cannon. 12 Fetlock. 13 Pastern. 14 Brisket. 15 Chestnut. 16 Flexor tendons. 17 Ergot. 18 Bulb of heel. 19 Chestnut. 20 Fetlock. 21 Hoof wall. 22 Coronet. 23 Shannon (shank). 24 Hock. 25 Point of hock. 26 Gaskin. 27 Hamstring. 28 Sheath. 29 Flank. 30 Point of buttock. 31 Hip. 32 Hindquarters. 33 Dock. 34 Croup. 35 Point of croup. 36 Loin. 37 Withers. 38 Crest. 39 Mane. 40 Atas. 41 Poll.

Knowledge of the points of the horse is vital for a real understanding of the animal. Experts acquire this by visual examination and physical touch. By feeling the point of the shoulder and other associated features, for instance, it is possible for them to establish what the actual angle of the shoulder is and so whether it is correctly conformed. An upright shoulder is often an indication that the horse lacks physical endurance. A backward-sloping shoulder means that the horse will have a longer stride and so be able to cover the ground more easily.

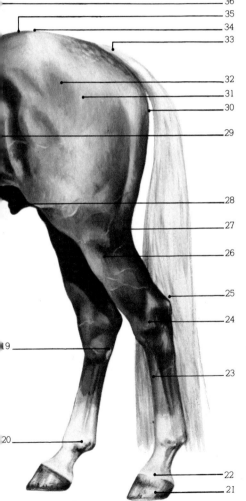

should be in a straight line, with the knees evenly placed. Otherwise the knee will be subjected to additional, unwanted strain.

The final feature of the forelegs are the so-called chestnuts — small, horny growths on the inside leg above the knee. These are thought to be vestiges of a former digit and, like fingerprints, each horse's are unique. Their presence is a survival from the distant past.

The body

Running from and supporting the withers — the ridge-like part of the dorsal spine between neck and back — the shoulder should be long and sloping. The greater the slope, the more efficient the shoulder is at absorbing concussion from the forelegs. An upright shoulder can make a horse an uncomfortable ride; endurance, too, can also be reduced, as the length of the stride is considerably shortened.

The breast lies to the front of the chest, between the forelegs. It should be broad and muscular, indicating that there is plenty of heart and lung-room behind it. Narrow-breasted horses invariably lack stamina, while there is the additional problem of trouble with the forelegs if these are set too close together. The neck should be straight and not unduly weighty, since this affects the carriage of the head. On no account should the angle at which the head is set on the neck be too acute, as otherwise the horse's breathing may be restricted.

The size of the head should be in proportion to the total size of the horse; if the head is too big, the forehand will be placed under extra strain. The muzzle should be well-defined, as should the nostrils. Eyes should be large, generous and clear, with uniformly curved lids, while ears should be well-pricked, alert and not over large.

The Points of the Horse

The left side of a mare and the right side of a stallion (below). The mare's complex anatomical make-up includes the following organs: **1** Aorta **2** Left lobe of liver. **3** Stomach. **4** Spleen. **5** Left kidney. **6** Body of uterus. **7** Oesophagus. **8** Trachea. **9** Left vagus nerve. **10** Left ventricle. **11** Left dorsal colon. **12** Small intestine. **13** Left ventral colon. **14** External anal sphincter muscle. **15** Vulva. **16** Urinary bladder. The stallion's include: **1** Right lobe of liver. **2** Right ventricle of heart. **3** Urinary bladder. **4** Rectum. **5** Descending duodenum. **6** Right kidney. **7** Azygos vein. **8** Right testicle. **9** Body of penis. **10** Lateral caecal band. **11** Dorsal sac of caecum. **12** Right ventral colon. **13** Caudal vena cava. Three features make the horse's digestive system unique. The first is that the greatest amount of the alimentary tract — the caesum and colon — is at the rear. The second is the small stomach and the third the lack of a gall bladder.

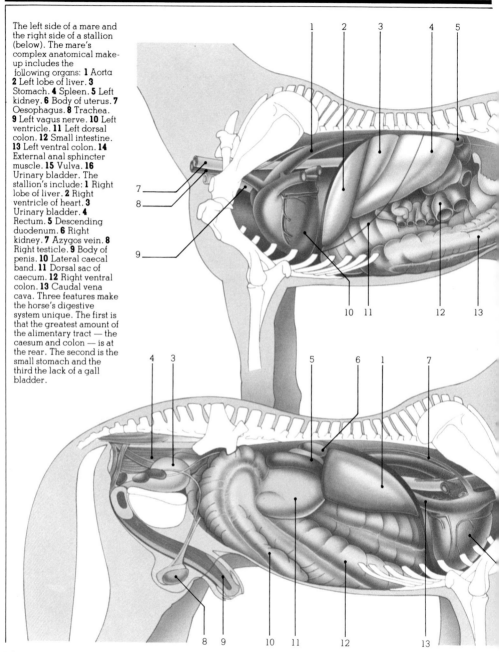

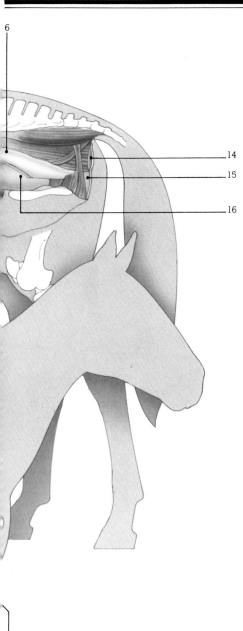

6

14

15

16

2

Droopy ears mean that the horse may be sluggish; long ears are often a sign of speed.

Between the ears lies the poll, leading to the top of the neck and the crest, which runs down to the withers and back. In general, the shorter the back, the stronger it will be — this is especially important since the back has to carry the rider's full weight. However, some experts prefer long-backed horses, provided that the horse is what is known as well 'ribbed up'. This means that the distance between the last rib and the point of the hip should not be greater than approximately 50 mm (2 in). The point of the hip itself projects outwards on either side of the backbone above the flanks. This is another possible injury spot, as the projection is relatively unprotected.

Behind the back lies the loin, which extends to the croup, or rump. This leads down to the tail and the dock. The loin should be strong and well-muscled, since it carries the propulsive power to the trunk. It should also be as short as possible, as it is the least supported part of the back. The croup is part of a general feature — the quarters — which also includes, buttock, hip, thigh and stifle. The quarters should be strong and straight, reaching well down into the second thighs. Rounded quarters — technically known as appley quarters — are undesirable.

The flank extends downwards from the lumbar spine. Its most prominent physical feature is at its highest point, just below the loin. This is a triangular indentation called the 'hollow of the flank'. As well as showing through its rise and fall how quickly or slowly the horse is breathing, the condition of the flank also acts as a good guide to the general condition of the horse. If the horse

19

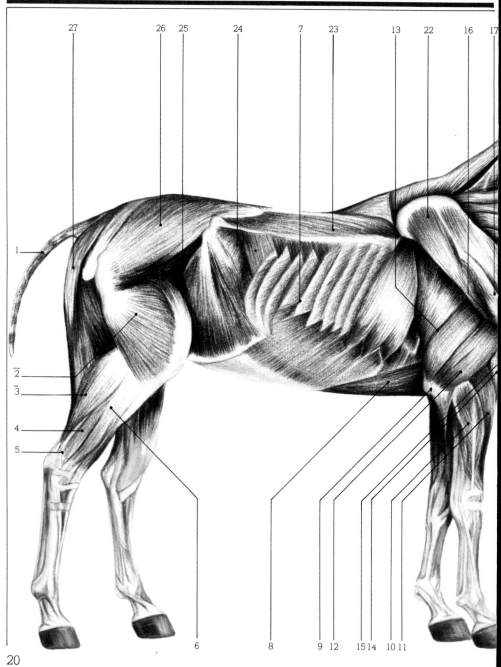

27 26 25 24 7 23 13 22 16 17

1

2
3
4
5

6 8 9 12 15 14 10 11

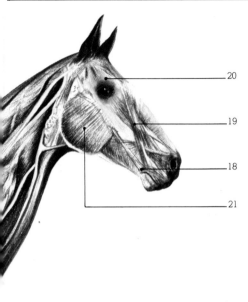

is unwell, it will probably be distended or 'tucked up'.

Internal organs

Most of the horse's internal organs work in the same way as those of other mammals, but both the digestive and respiratory systems have features of interest. In the digestive system, in particular, there are three unique features which distinguish the horse from other mammals. These are that the greatest volume of the alimentary tract is at the rear, where the major digestive processes take place; that the stomach is very small for the animal's size; and that there is no gall bladder. The reason for this is probably because the animal needs a constant supply of bile, as it is a continuous feeder.

Three points about the respiratory system are worth noting, since they are connected with the risk of illness or injury.

The principal muscles of the horse. 1 Tail depressors. 2 Lateral vastus. 3 Gastrocnemius. 4 Lateral digital extensor. 5 Deep digital flexor. 6 Long digital extensor. 7 External intercostal. 8 Caudal deep pectoral. 9 Point of elbow. 10 Common digital extensor. 11 Radial carpal extensor. 12 Lateral head of triceps. 13 Long head of triceps. 14 Brachialis. 15 Biceps brachii. 16 Teres minor. 17 Scapular spine. 18 Orbicularis oris. 19 Levator muscle of upper lip and nostril wing. 20 Corrugator supercilii. 21 Masseter. 22 Supraspinatus. 23 Longissimus dorsi. 24 Retractor costae. 25 Iliacus. 26 Medial gluteal. 27 Semitendinosus.

In the outer hindlimb there are the following tendons, as well as muscles. 1 Achilles tendon. 2 Superficial flexor tendon. 3 Deep flexor tendon. 4 Common digital extensor tendon.

In the outer forelimb: 5 Lateral digital extensor. 6 Superficial flexor tendon. 7 Deep flexor tendon. 8 Common digital extensor tendon. 9 Suspensory ligament. The muscles and tendons of the legs are vital to the horse's survival, but both are prone to injury. Tendons transfer the power produced by muscular contraction to the appropriate bones and joints. They run down the leg; the muscles are grouped together at the top. Each consists of thousands of fibres, lying in connective tissue, surrounded by a smooth membrane and sheath, and lubricated by fluid.

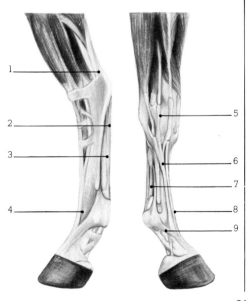

The guttural pouches of the head, for instance, can be infected or become the site of bleeding, while the larynx can become paralyzed on one side. This paralysis obstructs the intake of air and leads to the condition known as roaring. This is particularly noticeable at speed. So, too, is the condition known as broken wind, which is involved with the bronchioles and the alveoli in the lungs.

Teeth and age

The age of a horse is determined by an examination of the six incisor (tearing) teeth in each jaw. In common with other mammals, the horse has two sets of teeth during its life; the first deciduous, or milk, teeth are replaced by permanent teeth as the animal matures, the process usually starting at the age of three and being completed by the age of five. The central teeth erupt first, followed by the laterals and finally by the corners.

The two central incisors are cut when the foal is only four weeks old — they may even be present at birth — and are followed by the laterals and corners at six week and six to nine month intervals respectively. The milk teeth are white, as opposed to the yellow of the permanent teeth, and taper towards the base.

With the complete emergence of the permanent teeth, other considerations have to be taken into account when determining age. By six, the corner incisors will have worn level; by the age of seven, they will have developed a hook shape — the 'seven year hook'. This disappears by the age of eight. At seven, too, the dark line known as the dental star begins to develop; by nine, this is visible on the biting edges of the teeth.

It is now that Galvayne's groove, a longitudinal furrow, appears on the upper corner incisors near the gum. The growth of this groove serves as one indication of increasing age; another is the increasing slope of the teeth, which reaches its climax between the ages of twenty and twenty-five. By the age of fifteen, Galvayne's groove will be halfway down the tooth, while, at twenty, it should have reached the lower edge. From this time onwards, however, it starts to disappear at the same speed as it first appeared. By the age of thirty, it will have vanished completely.

All these points make it possible to determine the age of a horse with reasonable accuracy. However, after the

Skeletal diagrams show three stages of the gallop (left) and the three stages of jumping (right). Hock and stifle joints play a vital role in both movements. In the gallop, their action gathers up the hind legs at the moment of suspension, while in the jump they power the spring at take-off and gather the hind legs up to clear the obstacle.

age of eight — when the horse is said to be aged — these methods are not always certain; this is particularly the case after fifteen.

The paces of the horse

The four basic paces of the horse are the walk, trot (jog in Western riding), canter (lope in Western riding) and gallop. In addition, US saddle horses have the extra gaits of pace, stepping pace, slow gait and rack.

As officially defined by the International Equestrian Federation (FEI), the walk is a marching pace in which the four legs of the horse follow each other in four time. The sequence of legs is left fore, right hind, right fore and left hind — two or three legs always being on the ground. The beats of the pace must be well-accented, even and regular or the walk is considered to be disunited or broken. The pace itself is sub-divided into medium, collected, extended and free.

The trot is a two-time pace on alternate diagonals (near fore and off hind and vice versa) separated by a moment of suspension. In other words, the diagonal hind and forelegs move together, the right foreleg and left hind leg leaving the ground before the left fore and right hind return to it. There are four recognized gaits — working, medium, collected and exten-

ded. The rider either rises in the saddle (posts) or remains seated.

Two faults are if the pace is too hurried, so that the forelegs reach the ground before the hinds, or if the hindlegs are dragged. In both cases the result is a four-time pace. A further fault is if one hind leg is brought further forward than the other one.

The canter is a three-time pace, in which the horse bounds forward with either the left or right foreleg leading depending on the direction being taken. In the right canter, for instance, the following sequence must be followed: left hind, left diagonal (right hind and left fore) and right fore. This is followed by a moment of suspension with all four legs in the air before the next stride forwards is taken. The recognized canters are working, medium, collected and extended.

The commonest fault is if the wrong leg leads; in such a case, the canter is termed 'disunited.'

The gallop — the horse's fastest pace — is a four-beat gait. It is a flat-out version of the canter, the chief difference being that the strides and the period of suspension are both much longer. The legs are raised in either of the following sequences — left fore, right fore, left hind and right hind, or the reverse.

A well-trained horse should make the transitions between the various paces

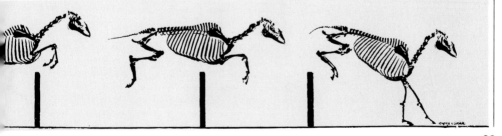

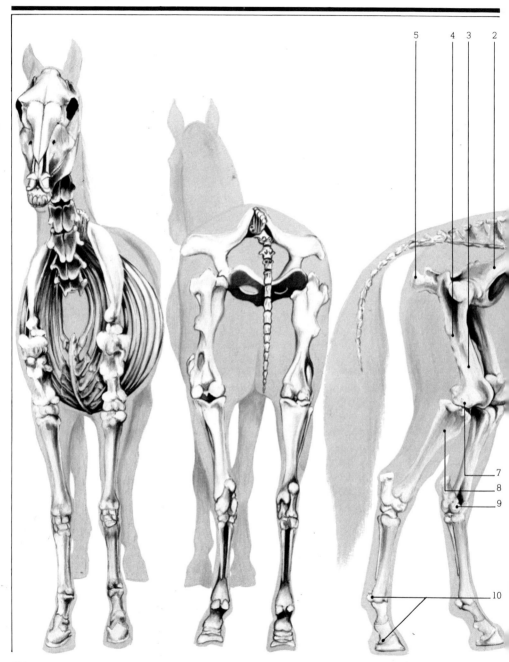

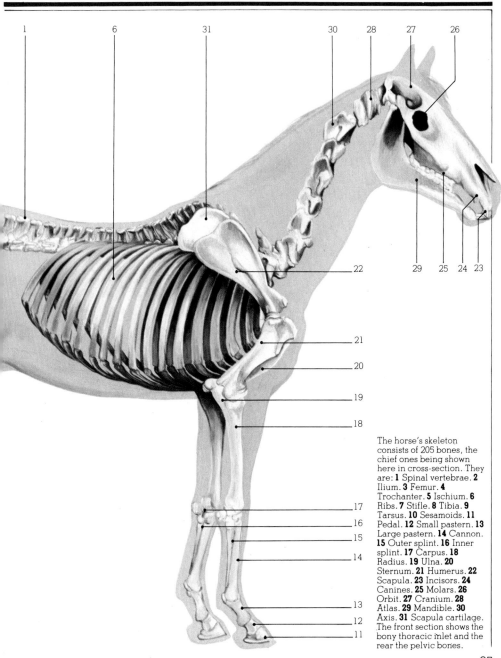

The horse's skeleton consists of 205 bones, the chief ones being shown here in cross-section. They are: **1** Spinal vertebrae. **2** Ilium. **3** Femur. **4** Trochanter. **5** Ischium. **6** Ribs. **7** Stifle. **8** Tibia. **9** Tarsus. **10** Sesamoids. **11** Pedal. **12** Small pastern. **13** Large pastern. **14** Cannon. **15** Outer splint. **16** Inner splint. **17** Carpus. **18** Radius. **19** Ulna. **20** Sternum. **21** Humerus. **22** Scapula. **23** Incisors. **24** Canines. **25** Molars. **26** Orbit. **27** Cranium. **28** Atlas. **29** Mandible. **30** Axis. **31** Scapula cartilage. The front section shows the bony thoracic inlet and the rear the pelvic bones.

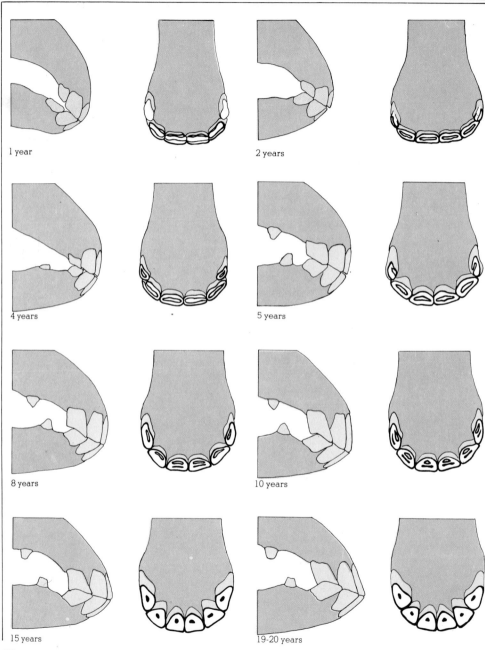

1 year

2 years

4 years

5 years

8 years

10 years

15 years

19-20 years

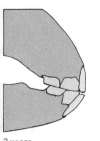

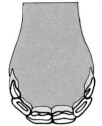

3 years

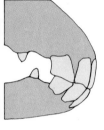

6 years

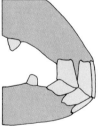

12 years

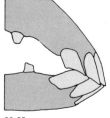

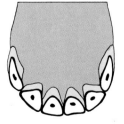

20-25 years

quickly and smoothly, not abruptly. The cadence, or rhythm, of the pace should be maintained up to the moment of the change or the halt. The horse should remain calm, light in hand and in the correct position at all times. Bad faults include grinding the teeth and swishing the tail, both being obvious signs of resistance.

Markings and colours

Markings are areas of white on the body, limbs and head of the horse. The terms used to describe them have been officially laid down by the various breeding authorities. On the body these are zebra marks (stripes on the limbs, neck, withers or quarters); and whorls (patterns of hairs around a small central point). Markings on the leg are either socks (white on the fetlock and part of the cannon) or stockings (white stretching from coronet to knee or hock). Socks are always shorter than the stockings.

On the head, markings are a star (a small white patch on the forehead); a stripe (a white line running down the face); a blaze (a broad white line from eyes to muzzle); a

An adult horse has a total of 40 teeth — three incisors, one canine (in colts and geldings) and six cheek teeth (three pre-molars and three molars) on the left and right sides of the upper and lower jaws. The chisel-like front teeth work with the animal's mobile lips when grazing; the back teeth, with their flat top surface criss-crossed with sharp enamel ridges, are ideally suited to grinding the food down.

Horses have two sets of teeth — milk and permanent. These are used to judge the animal's age. Up to five, the gradual emergence of the permanent teeth is the chief guide. At six, the corner incisors have worn level; by seven, they will have developed the 'seven year hook'. At this age, too, the dark dental star begins to develop; by nine it can be seen on the biting edges of the teeth. Simultaneously with this, the longitudinal furrow known as Galvayne's groove starts to emerge on the upper corner incisors. Its growth serves as an indication of age up to twenty; so, too, does the increasing slope of the teeth. However, after fifteen, accuracy is difficult.

27

white face (forehead, eyes, nose and parts of the muzzle); a snip (a small white line running into or around the nostril); and wall eye (blue-white or white colouring in the eye).

Colours of the horse vary widely. They range from bay (brownish horse chestnut, with a black mane, tail and, usually, black lower legs); black (coat, limbs, mane and tail with white points, if any); brown (brown to black points); chestnut (varying shades of red, ranging from dark to liver and light, the last sometimes being termed sorrel); dun (blue or yellow, with black points, dorsal stripe, mane and tail); cream (with light mane and tail and, often, pink eyes); palomino (golden, with flaxen mane and tail); roan (blue or strawberry, the former having black or brown as the basic colour with a touch of white and the latter with chestnut as the base); piebald (black and white); skewbald (red or chestnut or bay and white); pinto (piebald, skewbald or odd-coloured); to grey (white and black on a black skin). This last colour alone has many individual variations — flea-bitten grey and iron grey being two common examples.

Colours and markings are usually listed in any sale document, together with details of type, breeding, age, height and character. The last is a particularly important heading; under it should follow brief descriptions of the mouth, manners, movement and type of ride of the horse concerned. Here it is a good idea to have stated how the horse behaves in traffic — particularly if the intended rider is to be a child.

Measuring height
The height of the horse is measured from the highest point of the withers to the

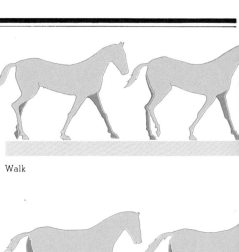

Walk

Trot

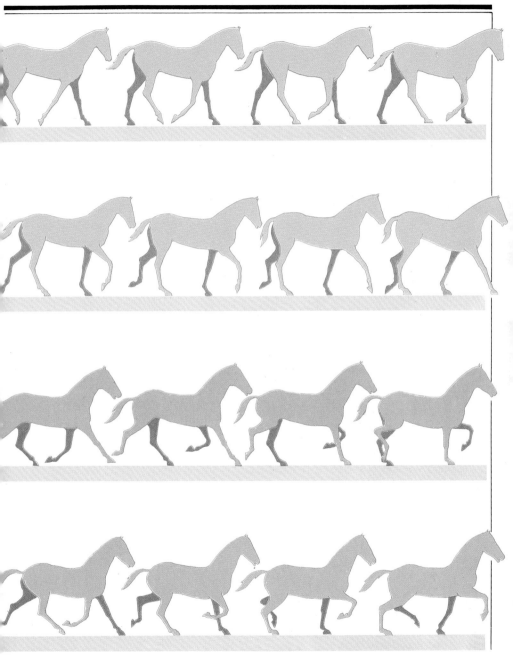

ground. For accuracy, it is important that the animal is standing square on a flat surface.

On the European continent, height is measured in centimetres, while in the UK, Ireland, Australasia and North America it is measured in hands. A hand is officially defined as 10.16 cm (4 in), which is the average distance across a man's knuckles; 15 hands 2 inches, or 15.2 hands, is the accepted way of setting out a fractionalised measurement. The abbreviation *hh* stands for 'hands high'.

Canter

The horse's mind

Leaving aside obvious faults of conformation — many of these are usually present at birth and are often impossible to eliminate fully — few horses are bad. If they are, they have generally been made so by faulty handling, training or inconsiderate riding. In this connection, it is important to realize that, compared to the size of its body, the horse has a small, relatively undeveloped, brain. The animal cannot reason and should not be credited with a human-type intelligence. What the horse does possess is a considerable degree of native instinct and this can be either utilized or marred by man.

Normally, what is required is patience and tact. If a horse shys at the unexpected, punishment will only serve to establish fear in the animal's mind. In the same way, wilfull misbehaviour should always be dealt with immediately — otherwise punishment will not be associated with the crime — while good behaviour should be immediately rewarded.

Gallop

A fit, well-fed, carefully-handled horse, however, will seldom have to face these or indeed any other major problems. It will be a pleasure to ride and to own.

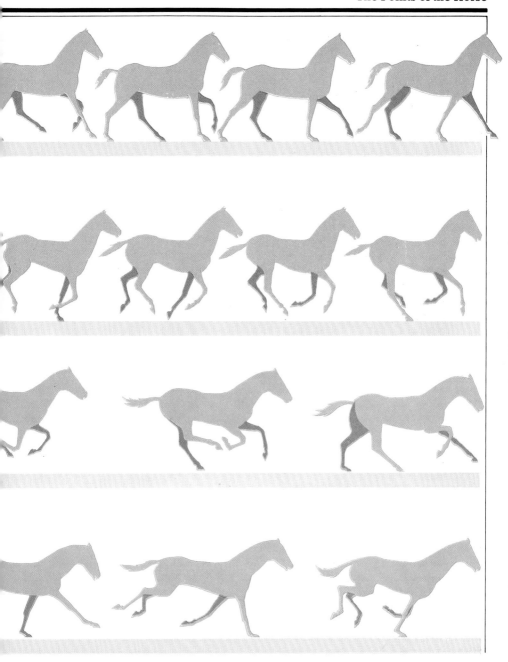

The Breeds of the World

There are literally hundreds of breeds of horse in the world today and their number and composition is constantly changing. There are many reasons for this; a breed can die out because the environment changes, for instance, or because it is no longer useful to man. The latter fate now threatens many of the breeds of heavy horses, whose work is now largely done by machine.

This decline, however, has been partly compensated for by growth in other parts of the horse world. With the great increase in the number of people riding for pleasure in the last twenty years, many countries have started stud books for riding horses to meet the growing demand. These books are divided into two main types. Many are 'open' — that is, the stallion and mare concerned need not be necessarily of the same breed, though they must both be pedigree stock. Others are 'closed'. This means that the offspring can only be registered if the parents are both members of the same breed.

A further means of definition is whether an animal is classed as a hotblood, warmblood, coldblood or pony. Hotbloods are pure-bred, fiery pedigree horses — the English Thoroughbred is a good example. Coldbloods are the heavy horses, the work horses of the world. The warmbloods are lighter animals, usually riding horses, which frequently have both coldblood and warmblood ancestry. Ponies are the small breeds — those which are under 14.2 hands in height — and are the particular favourites of children.

There are, however, certain anomalies within the system. Types, such as Hunter, Hack and Cob, are not registered in the stud books, though a registered Thoroughbred can, of course, be a Hunter. Horses such as the Australian feral Brumby, too, are difficult to place. The Brumby is not a recognized breed — nor is it a type — yet it has been crossbred with domestic stock to produce recognized offspring.

Middle East and Africa

Two of the most influential horses in the world — the Arab and the Barb — originated in these two areas. Though there is some dispute over the Arab's exact origins, the majority opinion is that it first ran wild in the Yemen in the Arabian peninsula. These early horses proved prepotent — that is, they passed their classic qualities of speed, toughness and stamina on from one generation to the next — and today Arab breeding is a world-wide industry. In the Middle East, the most important are the Persian and the Egyptian; the former plays an important role in Iran's horse-breeding programme, which also utilizes imported Thoroughbreds and native Turkomans. Most other Iranian strains are covered under one stud book, that of the Plateau Persian. Neighbouring Turkey, too, at one time produced fine Arabs, but a decline in quality meant the importation of the Nonius from Hungary to improve them and breed the Karacabey.

The Barb comes from North Africa. It is

distinguished from the Arab by the different appearance of its head, the lower set of its tail and its more fiery temperament. Frequent crossing over the centuries, however, means that few pure-bred Barbs survive today. In South Africa, there is only one native horse — the Basuto Pony.

Australia and East Asia

Australia's domestic horses are all descended from ones brought to the country by the first British settlers in the 1790s (the Brumby is descended from some which escaped to roam wild). The first major native breed was the Waler, so-called because it was first bred in New South Wales. Formed by crossing Arab, Thoroughbred and Anglo-Arab stallions with local mares and cobs, the breed was the chief source of remounts for the British army in India in the nineteenth century; however, it was not until 1971 that a stud book was finally formed. The animal was then rechristened the Australian Stock Horse. The Australian Pony's stud book was started in 1929. In addition to these, many Thoroughbreds, trotters and Arabs are bred.

This activity is all part and parcel of Australia's flourishing horse industry. From the start, the country proved to be an excellent one for rearing horses, as New Zealand did later. Today, from originally having been importers, both nations are now major exporters.

Throughout East Asia, there are many exotic breeds. These include the Indian Manipur (a type rather than a true breed), which was the first polo pony when the game was taken up by Europeans. China is the home of the oldest surviving breed of horse — the Mongolian Wild Horse, discovered by Colonel Przewalski in 1881 — while among Indonesia's ponies is the romantic Sumba. This is bred as a dancing pony.

The USSR

It was in about 3000 BC that the horse was first domesticated — this momentous event taking place within the boundaries of the present-day USSR. Since that time, horses have played a major role in the region's development. Because of the vast geographic area involved, many different types and breeds have evolved — the Arab having the chief influence in the west and the Mongolian Wild Horse to the east. Today the state authority recognizes forty breeds and breed groups.

Two of the most important of these are the Akhal Teké and the Orlov Trotter. The Akhal Teké is descended from the ancient Turkoman horses and is noted for its powers of endurance. The Orlov Trotter is of more recent origin. It was first bred in 1877 by Count Orlov by crossing an Arab stallion with a Dutch/Danish mare. The product was later refined to produce the Russian Trotter.

This process of refinement is now official breeding policy and is carried out by crossing existing stock with outside breeds. The Don, for example, has had Thoroughbred and Arab blood added; it itself was used to toughen other breeds.

In addition, new breeds have been developed, while, at the same time, some of the celebrated nineteenth-century breeds have been allowed to die out — though not before being used as foundation stock for their replacements. Thus the Strelets (a large Arab) was used as a basis for the Tersky (established 1948), and the Klepper (a tough preponent pony) for the Toric and Viatka.

Eastern Europe

Out of all the countries in Europe, Poland has the largest horse population; today it stands at about 3 million. Over the centuries, many different types of horse have been bred for a variety of uses, but a constant factor has been the influence of Arab blood. The Wielkopolski, for instance, has Arab, Thoroughbred and Trakehner ancestry. It is one of the many products of the state studs, whose other successes include the world-famous Polish Arab.

The oldest surviving native pony is the Tarpan, whose origins go back to the Ice Age. However, the modern Tarpan is an act of skillful recreation. Its influence is also seen in the Huçul and the Konik, the latter being the foundation stock for many other breeds.

Hungary's horse-breeding history, too, shows Arab influence. The tough horses of the early Magyars were later cross-bred with Arabs to produce many famous types, the most celebrated being the Shagya. This, in turn, played a vital part in the foundation of the Lipizzaner. Other major influences were the British Thoroughbreds which were used in the founding of the Furioso strain. A French stallion produced the Nonius.

Czechoslovakia and Bulgaria are also important horse centres. The former has the oldest operational stud in the world at Kladruby, where the white Kladrubers are bred. Bulgaria produces three well-known half-breds — the Pleven, the Danubian and the East Bulgarian — while Yugoslavia's most important native

product is the Bosnian Pony.

Scandinavia

The demands of war played a part in the development of two of Denmark's best-known horses. The Jutland — today a work horse — carried many medieval knights into battle; the Frederiksborg, bred from a mixture of Andalusian, Neapolitan, Arab and British blood in the sixteenth century, similarly served as a charger.

Other Danish horses are the Fjord Pony and a relatively recent innovation, the Danish Sports Horse.

Sweden has the Swedish Halfbred — a good dressage and eventing horse — the Swedish Ardennes as a work horse and the Gotland as its native pony. The Norwegian pony is the Norwegian Fjord, while the country also produces the Døle and the Døle Trotter. Finland has the Finnish Horse and Iceland the Icelandic Pony.

Switzerland, Austria, Belgium Holland

The most celebrated Austrian horse is without question the Lipizzaner, the world-famous mounts used by the Spanish Riding School in Vienna. Spanish blood, too, played a major part in the founding of the breed; it was first bred at the stud founded by the Archduke Charles in 1580 at Lipizza near Trieste. The horse's present breeding centre is at Piber in south Austria.

The other noted Austrian horses are the Halflinger and the Noriker. The latter was originally bred by the Romans. Home-produced half-breds, Hanoverians and Trakeheners are used to breed the Austrian Riding Horse.

The Belgian, together with the Ardennes, are Belgium's chief work horses. The former is a direct descendant of the medieval Flanders Horse. The Belgium Warmblood is a more recent innovation. Neighbouring Holland has three native breeds — the Gelderland, the Gronigen and the Friesland — as well as stud books for Arabs, Hackneys, Dutch Warmbloods, Trotters, Race-horses and five pony breeds.

Switzerland's two historic horses are the Einsielder and the Freiberger. Since the 1960s, they have been joined by the Swiss Halfbred.

West and East Germany
West Germany is particularly noted for its fine riding horses, the best known of which are the Hanoverian, the Trakehner and the Holstein. The Hanoverian owes a great deal of its success to the English Thoroughbred blood introduced between 1714 and 1837. Its great rival, the Trakehner, had its original home in East Prussia, where the founding stud was established in 1732. In 1944, however, the advancing Soviet armies forced evacuation; 700 mares and a handful of stallions reached the west to form the nucleus of the present breed. The Holstein, for its part, has been bred in Schleswig-Holstein since the fourteenth century.

All other German warmbloods have used these three breeds as foundation stock, with other blood being added if necessary. German's heavy horses, the Rhineland and the Schleswig Heavy Draught, similarly owe a debt to imported stock.

East Germany's two leading breeds are the Mecklenburg and the East Frisian;
they are closely related to the Hanoverian and the Oldenburg respectively.

France
More than in any other Western country, the state dominates horse-breeding in France through the Service des Havas, which is responsible for the industry. The Service runs twenty-three stallion depots, which, in the best breeding areas, such as Normandy, house as many as 200 stallions.

The main competition horse is the Selle Francais, an amalgamation of forty-five different breed groups founded in 1965. Of these, the Anglo-Norman and Anglo-Arab were the most influential — Arabs, indeed, are the ancestors of all French breeds and are still extensively used for cross-breeding.

French Thoroughbreds and Trotters are world-famous, while the Percheron is the best-known heavy horse. Ponies include the Camargue, the Basque and the Landais.

Southern Europe
Italy's most famous horse was the medieval Neapolitan, which found its way into the royal courts of Europe as a high school horse and also became the foundation stock for many breeds. So, too, did the Andalusian, the most important of the horses of Spain. Nowadays, however, imported breeds dominate the Italian scene and native riding horses, such as the Murghese and Calabrese, are on the decline.

Portugal's breeds — the Altér-Real and the Lusitano — have close links with the Andalusian, as they have similar Arab and Barb ancestry. So, too, has the Minho pony; the other native Portuguese breed is the tough Sorraia. Greece's native stock consists of three ponies — the Peneia, Pindos and Skyros.

South America

The Criollo, the horse of the Argentinian *gaucho* (cowboy) is descended from a group of Andalusian horses brought by the Spanish to the New World, which escaped to roam wild. The Argentinian polo pony is a cross between it and the Thoroughbred, while Brazil's Crioulo is a smaller version of the Criollo. Other Brazilian horses of note are the Mangalarga and the Campolino, the latter being selectively bred from the former. Peru's Steeping Horse, with its unique lateral gait, gave rise to Puerto Rico's Paso Fino. Venezuela, like most South American countries, has its own version of the Criollo — the Llanero.

North America

Though North America was the original home of *Equus caballos,* horses died out there at the end of the Ice Age — not to reappear until the Spanish landed there in 1511. Some of these escaped to give the Indians their Mustangs, but the only Indian horse to be recognized as a breed is the Appaloosa. This was first bred by the Nez Perce tribe at the end of the eighteenth century.

Later colonists also brought horses with them and it was from these that the first native breeds emerged. The earliest of these was the Narrangansett Pacer; it was followed by the Quarter Horse, the oldest surviving US breed. Its name comes from the test of quality instituted by its Virginian breeders — racing it over a quarter of a mile. An all-purpose

animal, it proved suited to many tasks, chief amongst these being its use as a cow pony. It is also used in rodeos, for riding, racing and in shows. Another old-established US breed is the Morgan, so-called because its founding sire was owned by an inn keeper, Justin Morgan.

With the Thoroughbred and the Narrangansett Pacer, the Morgan was also the foundation stock for the Saddlebred, a spectacular horse with three or five smooth gaits. The Tennessee Walking Horse, officially recognized in 1935, has even smoother paces.

In more recent times, the US has defined breeds that do not, as yet, breed true on the basis of colour. One such breed is the Palomino; others are the Indian Pinto and the Albino. The US native pony is the Pony of the Americas, developed in the 1960s. Imported horses, particularly Thoroughbreds, also play an extremely important role on the American scene.

Canada has no native horse breed, the Canadian Cutting Horse being defined as a type.

Britain and Ireland

Britain and Ireland have bred some of the finest horses in the world. The UK's greatest contribution has been the Thoroughbred, the world's fastest and most valuable breed whose origins date back to the seventeenth and eighteenth centuries. Starting from around 1660, more than 200 Arab-type horses were imported to improve the native British racing stock. It is still uncertain whether these imported horses were crossed with native racing mares — the now extinct Galloway ponies — or whether the foundations were purely Oriental. There is no question, however, that the three greatest influences were the stallions Darley Arabian, Byerley Turk and Godolphin Barb. The first was the originator of the Blandford, Phalaris, Gainsborough, Son in Law and St Simon lines, the second of the Herod line and the third of the Matcham line.

Arab blood, too, has played an important part in the development of the Welsh Mountain Pony, which is officially described as 'an Arab in miniature'. Similarly, the eye-catching Hackney Horse, with its spectacular high-stepping trot, combines Yorkshire Hackney and Arab blood. There are also traces of the now extinct Norfolk Trotter in its ancestry.

The UK's other main contribution to the horse world has been its native ponies. These have a long history, dating back to the original wild stock that roamed moor, forest and fell.

Nine native breeds of pony now exist, of which the Exmoor is probably the oldest. Its presence is recorded in the Domesday Book, but its origins go back far further – to prehistoric times when the remote ancestors of the Exmoors crossed the land bridge that then linked Britain and the Continent. Its neighbour, the Dartmoor, is bigger and not as pure bred. Further to the east, the New Forest Pony has had additions of Arab, Thoroughbred and Galloway blood. Among the doners of Arabs was Queen Victoria, who in 1852 lent a stallion to improve the breed. This ran wild with the mares for eight years and was followed by two more — also donated by the Queen — in 1885. The result was a well proportioned, sure footed riding pony, standing about 14 hh, with an easy action and a good temperament.

The Pennines are the home of the Fell Pony; its neighbour to the east — the Dale — is the largest of Britain's native pony breeds. Across the border in Scotland, the Highland shares a common ancestry with the Fell and the Dale. However, additions of Arab and French blood have led to the emergence of two quite distinct varieties — the Highland Pony and the Highland Garron. The latter is bigger and stronger than the former.

Even further to the north lies the island home of the Shetland Pony. The ancestry of the small but sturdy breed dates back to around 500 BC, when ponies were introduced to the Shetlands from Scandinavia. Subsequently, these ponies were probably crossed with animals brought from the mainland by the Celts.

The only recognized British riding/ driving horse is the Cleveland Bay, which has been bred in Yorkshire for over two hundred years. The largest British horse is the Shire, which is probably a descendant of the medieval Great Horse. So, too, is the Scottish Clydesdale. The slightly smaller Suffolk Punch originated in the 1760s.

Ireland's horse industry plays a major part in the country's economic life and many of the horses bred there become world-beaters, particularly in the racing field. On the west coast, the tough, handsome Connemara Pony still roams wild, as it has done for centuries. In origin, it probably has the same ancestry as the Highland; the chief difference lies in the injection of Spanish blood the Connemara received from the horses and ponies that swam ashore after the shipwreck of the Spanish Armada in 1588.

Akhal Teké

Akhal Teké

Warmblood
Origin Turkoman Steppes.
Height 15 hands.
Colour bay, chestnut, grey
or black, usually with
metallic sheen.
Physique elegant, long
head, straight profile,
long, thin neck, long back,
low-set silky tail, long legs
with light, strong bone.
Features hardy,
temperamental, fast and
versatile.
Temperament bold, but
can be obstinate.
Use riding.

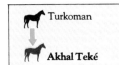

Albino

Warmblood
Origin USA.
Height any.
Colour white with pink
skin, pale blue or dark
brown eyes.
Physique lightweight
frame, otherwise varies.
Temperament kindly,
intelligent.
Use riding.

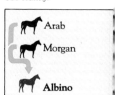

Altér Real

Altér Real

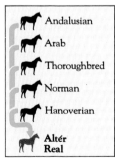

🐎 Andalusian

🐎 Arab

🐎 Thoroughbred

🐎 Norman

🐎 Hanoverian

🐎 **Altér Real**

Warmblood
Origin Alentejo province, Portugal.
Height 15.2 hands.
Colour chestnut, bay or piebald.
Physique smallish head with straight profile, short, arched neck, close-

coupled, strong loins and hindquarters and good, fine bone.
Features extravagant high knee action.
Temperament intelligent,

highly-strung, brave.
Use riding, especially high school equitation.

39

Andalusian

Andalusian

Warmblood
Origin Andalusia.
Height 16 hands.
Physique largish head,
almost convex profile,
strong, arched neck,
deep, short-coupled body
round hindquarters and
short cannon bones.

Features athletic, great
presence, an elegant,
springy action.
Temperament intelligent,
affectionate.
Use high school
equitation, general riding.

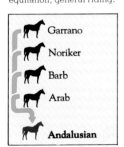

Garrano

Noriker

Barb

Arab

Andalusian

40

Anglo-Arab

Anglo-Arab

good movement.
Temperament brave,
sweet-tempered, intelligent.
Use riding, competitions
and racing.

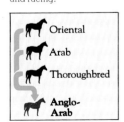

Warmblood
Origin Britain, France and
Poland.
Height 16 hands.
Colour solid colours.
Physique good shoulder
and well-proportioned,
powerful hindquarters.
Features stamina and

41

Appaloosa

Appaloosa

Warmblood
Origin western USA.
Height 15 hands.
Colour six basic patterns
of spots usually on roan or
white, white sclera around
eye.
Physique short-coupled
thin mane and tail, hard

feet which are often
striped.
Features striking
appearance.
Temperament tractable,
hardy with great
endurance.
Use as a cow pony, a
pleasure and parade horse
and in the circus.

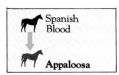

Spanish
Blood

Appaloosa

Arab

Arab

Thoroughbred.
Origin Arabia.
Height 14.3 hands.
Colour bay, chestnut, grey.
Physique small, tapering head, concave face, broad forehead, large, dark eyes, small ears, arched neck, long, sloping shoulder, short straight back, straight croup, high-set tail, fine legs but very hard bone.
Features fast free-floating action, stamina and toughness.
Temperament spirited, enduring intelligent, bold.
Use improving other breeds, long distance and general riding.

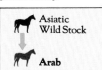

Asiatic Wild Stock

Arab

Ardennais

Ardennais

Coldblood
Origin France — Lorraine Champagne, foothills of Vosges.
Height 15.3 — 16 hands.
Colour bay, chestnut or roan.
Physique short, stocky compact, heavyweight,

with a large bone structure, strong head and broad face.
Features hardy.
Temperament docile, gentle and willing.
Use agriculture.

Ardennes

Coldblood
Origin Belgium — the Ardennes.
Height 15.3 hands
Colour bay, chestnut or roan.
Physique muscular, short-coupled body, crested neck, broad chest and short, feathered legs.
Features strong, active.

Temperament gentle and willing.
Use agriculture.

Australian Pony

Pony.
Origin Australia.
Height 13 hands.
Colour most colours.
Physique Arab head,

Australian Stock Horse

longish neck, sloping shoulder, deep girth, round hindquarters.
Temperament intelligent, enduring, courageous.
Use riding.

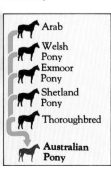

Arab

Welsh Pony

Exmoor Pony

Shetland Pony

Thoroughbred

Australian Pony

Australian Stock Horse

Warmblood.
Origin New South Wales.
Height 16 hands.
Colour all colours.
Physique varies, usually alert head, deep girth, strong back.
Features hardy, with a

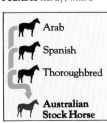

Arab

Spanish

Thoroughbred

Australian Stock Horse

strong constitution.
Temperament reliable, versatile, hard working.
Use herding and cavalry.

Avelignese

Pony.
Origin the Italian Alps and Appennines.

Height 14 hands.
Colour chestnut with flaxen mane and tail.
Physique heavy-frame, short, feathered legs and large, hard feet.
Features sure-footed and long-lived.
Temperament good-tempered, gentle, easy-to-train and tough.
Use pack work in the mountains, light agricultural work.

Oriental

Halflinger

Avelignese

Barb

Balearic

Temperament good, docile and patient.
Use agricultural work and driving.

Pony.
Origin Majorca.
Height about 14 hands.
Colour bay or brown.
Physique fine head, usually Roman nose, light, tough frame and hard feet.
Features free, graceful action.

Bali

Pony.
Origin Indonesia/Bali.
Height 12.2 hands.
Colour dun with dorsal.
stripe and dark points.
Physique sturdy frame.
Features frugal and
strong.
Temperament good
workhorse.
Use riding and general
pack work.

Barb

Warmblood.
Origin Algeria and
Morocco.
Height 14.2 hands.
Colour bay, brown,
chestnut, black and grey.
Physique long head,
straight profile, sloping
quarters, low-set tail and
long, strong legs. .
Features frugal and
tough.
Temperament docile and
courageous.

Use adding strength to
other breeds, such as the
Andalusian and
Thoroughbred, riding and
transport.

Bashkirsky

Pony.
Origin Bashkiria, USSR.
Height 13.2 hands.
Colour bay, dun or
chestnut.
Physique thickset,
prominent wither, longish
back, low-set tail and short
legs.
Features tough.
Temperament calm,
good-tempered and hardy.
Use riding and pulling
sleighs; mares are milked
for *kumiss*.

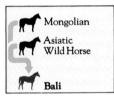

Basque

Pony.
Origin Basque region of
France.
Height 13 hands.
Colour most.
Physique primitive, with
head slightly concave,
small ears, short neck and
long back.
Features stamina and
toughness.
Temperament quick to
mature and enduring.
Use mining, riding.

Basuto

Basuto

Pony.
Origin South Africa.
Height 14.2 hands.
Colour chestnut, bay,
brown and grey.
Physique quality head,
longish neck and back,
strong, straightish
shoulder, short legs and

hard hooves.
Features sure-footed and
tough, with great stamina.
Temperament fearless
and self-reliant.
Use racing, polo and
riding.

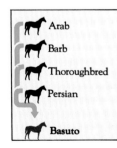

Batak

Pony.
Origin Sumatra,
Indonesia.
Height 12.2 hands.
Colour most colours.
Physique comparatively
refined, good
conformation.
Features frugal.

Temperament spirited.
good-tempered, handles
well.
Use agriculture and
transport.

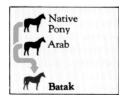

Belgian Heavy Draught

Bavarian

Warmblood.
Origin Lower Bavaria, West Germany.
Height 16 hands.
Colour solid colours.
Physique medium-sized frame, deep girth and broad chest.
Features derived from

Rottaler war horse.
Temperament sensible, docile and willing.
Use riding.

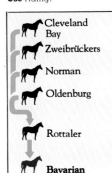

Cleveland Bay
Zweibrückers
Norman
Oldenburg
Rottaler
Bavarian

Belgian Heavy Draught

(Brabant)
Coldblood.
Origin Brabant.
Height 16.2 hands.
Colour red roan with black points, or chestnut.
Physique heavy, large

frame, shortish back, short legs with feather on fetlocks.
Features strength, presence and good action.
Temperament courageous and tractable.
Use draught work.

Flanders Horse
Ardennes
Ancient Forest Horse
Belgian

Bosnian

Bhutia

Temperament alert and
intelligent, but not always
good-tempered.
Use transportation in the
mountains.

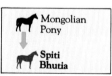

Pony.
Origin India.
Height 12 hands.
Colour grey.
Physique thickset and
short-coupled.
Features sure-footed and
tough.

Bosnian

Temperament tough,
affectionate and very
intelligent.
Use agricultural work.

Pony.
Origin Yugoslavia.
Height 12.2. hands.
Colour dun, brown, grey,
black or chestnut.
Physique compact
mountain pony.
Features endurance.

Breton

Boulonnais

Coldblood.
Origin Northern France.
Height 16.1 hands.
Colour grey, chestnut or
bay.
Physique similar to
Percheron, silky coat.
Features lively and active.

Temperament good
tempered, intelligent.
Use draught.

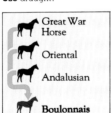

Great War
Horse

Oriental

Andalusian

Boulonnais

Breton
Coldblood.
Origin France.
Height 16.1 hands.
Colour grey, chestnut or
bay.
Physique Postier Breton;

close coupled, elegant
head and short legs with
little feather. Draught
Breton; larger, more
elongated body.
Features strong and
active, although the
Draught is less energetic.
Temperament sweet
tempered, lively and
willing.
Use agricultural work.

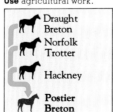

Draught
Breton

Norfolk
Trotter

Hackney

Postier
Breton

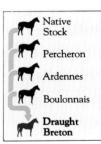

Native
Stock

Percheron

Ardennes

Boulonnais

**Draught
Breton**

Budyonny

Budyonny
(Budenny)

Warmblood.
Origin USSR.
Height 15.3 hands.
Colour chestnut or bay with golden sheen.
Physique strong frame, crested neck, close-coupled and deep bodied.
Features fast and enduring.
Temperament intelligent; calm and energetic.
Use riding, competitions and steeplechasing.

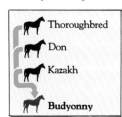

Thoroughbred
Don
Kazakh
Budyonny

Burma

Burma

Use polo and general.

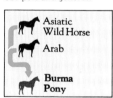

Pony.
Origin Burma.
Height 13 hands.
Colour all colours.
Physique thickset with high-set tail.
Features strong hill-pony.
Temperament active, but can be slow in response.

Calabrese

Warmblood.
Origin Calabria, Italy.
Height about 16 hands.
Colour solid colours.
Physique middleweight, short-coupled riding horse.
Features handsome saddle horse.

Temperament intelligent, easy to manage.
Use riding.

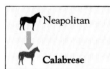

Camargue

Camargue
(Camarguais)

Pony.
Origin The Camargue,
Rhone delta, France.
Height 14 hands.
Colour grey.
Physique Oriental-type
head, straightish shoulder,
short body, fine legs with

hard bone.
Features hardy.
Temperament quiet and
reliable when broken.
Use herding, trekking,
also roams wild.

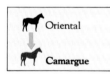

Campolino

Warmblood.
Origin Brazil.
Height 14.3-15 hands.
Physique similar to the
Mangalarga, but with a
heavier frame and more
bone.
Features hardy dual-
purpose horse.

Temperament tough,
willing and enduring.
Use riding and light
draught work.

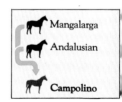

Canadian Cutting Horse

Canadian Cutting Horse

Features fast and agile.
Temperament quick
witted and intelligent.
Use competition and stock
work.

Warmblood.
Origin North America.
Height 15.2-16.1 hands.
Colour almost any colour.
Physique like the US
Quarter Horse, with long
body, short legs, powerful
hindquarters.

Caspian

Caspian Pony

Pony.
Origin Iran.
Height 10-11.2 hands.
Colour grey, brown, bay
or chestnut.
Physique Arab-type head,
fine boned.
Features sure-footed.

Temperament gentle,
tractable and intelligent,
ideal for children.
Use transport and riding.

56

Cleveland Bay

Cleveland Bay

Warmblood.
Origin Yorkshire.
UK.
Height 16 hands.
Colour bay or brown;
white markings not
desirable.
Physique large head,
convex profile, longish

back, high-set tail and
good bone.
Features versatile, strong
and long-lived.
Temperament intelligent,
calm and sensible.
Use riding and driving.

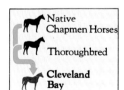

Clydesdale

Coldblood.
Origin Lanarkshire, UK.
Height 16.2 hands.
Colour dark with white on
face and legs.
Physique long, crested
neck high withers,
straightish hind legs,
much feather.

Features active.
Temperament brave and
friendly.
Use draught.

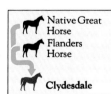

Connemara

Comtois

Coldblood.
Origin Franche Comté, France.
Height 15.1 hands.
Colour bay or chestnut.
Physique largish head, straight neck, long, straight back and little feather.

Features active and sure footed.
Temperament courageous, kind and willing.
Use agriculture.

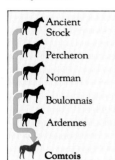

- Ancient Stock
- Percheron
- Norman
- Boulonnais
- Ardennes
- **Comtois**

Connemara

Pony.
Origin County Connaught, Eire.
Height 13.2 hands.
Colour grey.
Physique compact, intelligent head, crested neck, sloping shoulder and deep, strong, sloping

hindquarters.
Features sure-footed, hardy; a good jumper.
Temperament intelligent, tractable and kind, good with children.
Use riding and driving.

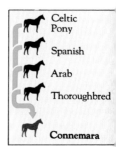

- Celtic Pony
- Spanish
- Arab
- Thoroughbred
- **Connemara**

Criollo

Criollo

Warmblood.
Origin Argentina.
Height 14.2 hands.
Colour dun with dark points, dorsal stripe with dark snippets; red and blue roan, sorrel and skewbald.
Physique short head

tapering to muzzle, short-coupled, sturdy frame, strong, sloping shoulder, short legs, good bone and small, hard feet.
Features tough and manoeuvrable.
Temperament willing, tough and enduring.
Use long-distance riding and ranch work.

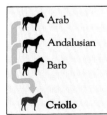

Crioulo

Warmblood.
Origin Brazil.
Height 15 hands.
Colour lighter Criollo colours.
Physique prominent withers, high-set tail and longish neck.
Features frugal and

tough.
Temperament enduring.
Use riding and herding.

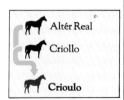

59

Dale

Dale

Pony.
Origin Eastern Pennines, UK.
Height 14.1 hands.
Colour dark colours, with no white except star.
Physique powerful frame, straightish shoulder, fine hair on heels and thick mane and tail.
Features strong (can pull one ton), sure-footed.
Temperament sensible, quiet and hard working.
Use pack, agricultural work and riding.

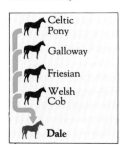

Danish Sport Horse

Warmblood.
Origin Denmark.
Height 16.1 hands.
Colour all colours.
Physique varies, middleweight build.
Features good general riding and competition horse.
Temperament versatile, competitive.
Use general riding.

- Hanoverian
- Native Halfbred
- Thoroughbred
- Trakehner
- Polish
- Anglo-Norman
- **Danish Sports Horse**

Dartmoor

Danubian

Warmblood.
Origin Bulgaria.
Height 15.2 hands.
Colour dark chestnut or
black.
Physique short-coupled,
deep girth, high-set tail
and fine strong legs.
Features strength.

Temperament active and
docile.
Use light draught, riding
and competitions.

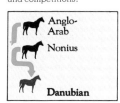

Dartmoor

Pony
Origin Dartmoor, Devon,
UK.
Height 12.1 hands.
Colour bay, black or
brown.
Physique small head,
strong shoulders, back
and loins, high-set tail and

full mane and tail.
Features long-lived, sure-
footed and tough.
Temperament kind and
sensible, ideal for
children.
Use riding.

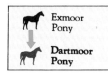

Døle

Døle

Warmblood.
Origin Norway.
Height 15 hands.
Colour black, brown or
bay.
Physique two types; heavy
draught — similar to the
UK Dale; pony type —
upright shoulder, deep

girth, short legs with good
bone and little feather.
Features tough, versatile.
Temperament active and
patient, adaptable.
Use agricultural work,
riding and driving.

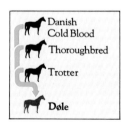

Døle Trotter

Warmblood.
Origin Norway.
Height 15 hands.
Colour black, brown or
bay.
Physique lighter version
of Dole with no feather.
Features good trotting
horse.

Temperament active,
tough and competitive.
Use trotting races.

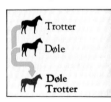

Don

Warmblood.
Origin Central Asia
(steppes).
Height 15.2 hands.
Colour chestnut, bay or
grey.

Don

Physique deep body,
long, straight neck and
back, long legs.
Features versatile, frugal,
with great stamina.
Temperament energetic,
calm and reliable.
Use the original Cossack
horse, now used for
driving, riding and long
distance racing.

Oriental

Thoroughbred

Orlov
Trotter

Turkoman

Karabakh

Karabair

Don

Dulmen

Pony.
Origin Westphalia.

Height 12.3 hands.
Colour black, brown or dun.
Physique various.
Features semi-wild breed.
Temperament hardy.
Use riding.

Dutch Draught

Cold blood.
Origin Holland.

Height 16.1 hands.
Colour bay, chestnut or
black.
Physique tall with a
powerful front and deep,
strong body.
Features strength and
stamina.
Temperament kind but
spirited, hard-working.
Use draught.

63

East Friesian

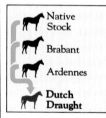

Native Stock

Brabant

Ardennes

Dutch Draught

East Bulgarian

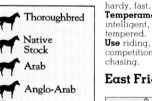

Thoroughbred

Native Stock

Arab

Anglo-Arab

East Bulgarian

Warmblood.
Origin Bulgaria.
Height 15.3 hands.
Colour chestnut or black.
Physique smallish head, straight profile, deep girth and longish, straight back.
Features energetic,

hardy, fast.
Temperament active, intelligent, good-tempered.
Use riding, agriculture, competitions and steeple chasing.

East Friesian

Warmblood.

Origin East Germany.
Height 16.1 hands.
Colour solid colours.
Physique similar to the Oldenburg but lighter, with a more elegant head.
Features quality saddle and carriage horse.
Temperament bold, kind and spirited.
Use riding and light draught work.

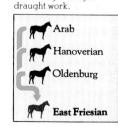

Arab

Hanoverian

Oldenburg

East Friesian

Exmoor

Egyptian Arab

Thoroughbred.
Origin Egypt..
Height 14.3 hands.
Colour grey.
Physique two types; the Kuhaylan is more rangey than the short-coupled Siglavy.
Features speed.

Temperament spirited and courageous, tough.
Use racing, breeding, general riding.

Einsiedler

Warmblood.
Origin Switzerland.
Height 16 hands.
Colour bay or chestnut.
Physique well-

proportioned, strong frame.
Features free action, energetic.
Temperament bold, intelligent, tractable and versatile.
Use riding and driving.

Ancient Stock

Hackney

Anglo-Norman

Einsiedler

Exmoor

Pony.
Origin Exmoor, Somerset and Devon, UK.
Height 12 hands.
Colour bay, brown or dun with black points, light mealy muzzle, no white.
Physique prominent 'toad' eyes, wide chest, strong

Falabella

quarters and thick,
springy coat with no bloom
in winter.
Features, strength and
endurance.
Temperament intelligent,
semi-wild, but good for
children if well-trained.
Use riding.

Falabella

Pony.
Origin Argentina.
Height 7 hands.
Colour all colours.
Physique the smallest
pony in the world.
Features hardy and full of
character.
Temperament friendly

and intelligent, an ideal
pet.
Use harness pony and pet.

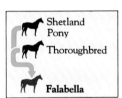

Finnish

Fell

Pony.
Origin Cumbria, UK.
Height 13.2 hands.
Colour black, brown or bay.
Physique great substance, minimum 8 inches of bone, fine hair on heels and long, curly mane and tail.

Features strength and stamina; a fast trotter.
Temperament lively and alert, a good worker.
Use all-purpose, driving agricultural work, pack and trekking.

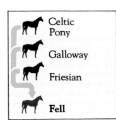

Celtic Pony

Galloway

Friesian

Fell

Finnish

Coldblood.
Origin Finland.
Height 15.2 hands.
Colour chestnut, bay and brown.
Physique short neck, upright shoulder, deep, strong legs, light feather.
Features tough, long-

lived, fast.
Temperament even-tempered, kind, gentle and quiet, yet lively and willing.
Use timber hauling, agriculture and trotting.

Indigenous Forest pony

Finnish Draught

Finnish

Finnish Universal

67

Fjord

Fjord

Pony.
Origin Norway.
Height 14 hands.
Colour dun, cream or
yellow with dorsal stripe
and upright black and
silver mane.
Physique small head,
strong, short neck and

powerful, compact body.
Features sure-footed, very
hardy.
Temperament gentle and
strong-willed, hard
working and tireless.
Use mountain work,
agriculture, transport,
riding and driving.

Asiatic
Wild Horse

Norwegian
Fjord Pony

Franches Montagnes

Franches Montagnes
(Freiberger)

Warmblood
Origin Avenche,
Switzerland.
Height 15.1 hands.
Colour blue roan or grey;
solid colours.

Physique powerful,
compact frame.
Features stamina,
strength.
Temperament active,
versatile and hard
working.
Use agricultural work.

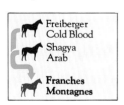

Freiberger
Cold Blood

Shagya
Arab

**Franches
Montagnes**

Fredericksborg

Fredericksborg

good-tempered and
willing.
Use light draught, riding.

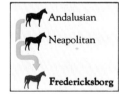

Warmblood.
Origin Denmark.
Height 15.3 hands.
Colour chestnut.
Physique strong, plain
harness horse, large chest,
strong back.
Features active.
Temperament tractable,

French Trotter

French Trotter

Features athletic and fast.
Temperament tough,
willing and competitive.
Use trotting, riding and
cross-breeding.

Warmblood
Origin Calvados.
Height 16.1 hands.
Colour any solid colour.
Physique tall, light-
framed horse with a fine
head, prominent wither,
strong back and sloping
hindquarters.

Friesian

Friesian

Warmblood
Origin Holland.
Height 15 hands.
Colour black.
Physique longish head, crested neck, round hindquarters, good bone, feather and full mane and tail.

Features great presence.
Temperament willing, good-tempered, hard-working.
Use circus, riding and driving, and all-round work horse.

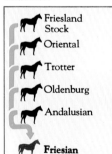

Friesland Stock

Oriental

Trotter

Oldenburg

Andalusian

Friesian

Furioso

Furioso

Warmblood
Origin Hungary.
Height 16 hands.
Colour dark colours.
Physique muscular body,
straightish back, sloping
hindquarters and low-set
tail.
Features robust.

Temperament active,
intelligent, tractable.
Use riding, competitions
driving and steeple-
chasing.

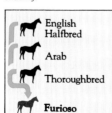

English
Halfbred

Arab

Thoroughbred

Furioso

Galiceno

Galiceno

Pony
Origin Mexico.
Height 12.2. hands.
Colour bay, black or dun.
Physique short-coupled, narrow frame.
Features versatile, natural running walk.
Temperament very

intelligent, versatile, brave and gentle.
Use ranch work and transportation.

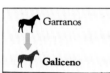

Garrano (Minho)

Pony
Origin Garranho do Minho, Traz dos Montes, Portugal.
Height 11 hands.
Colour dark chestnut.
Physique light frame, full mane and tail and good conformation.

Features strong and sure footed.
Temperament hardy, quick, good-tempered.
Use riding and pack.

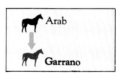

Gelderland

Gelderland

Warmblood
Origin Gelderland.
Height 15.1 hands.
Colour chestnut, or grey.
Physique plain head,
almost convex profile,
crested neck, short-
coupled with a high set
tail.

Features extravagant
action and great presence.
Temperament docile,
good tempered and active.
Use carriage work, light
agricultural work and
riding.

Gotland

Pony
Origin Gotland Islands,
Sweden.
Height 12.1 hands.
Colour dun, black, brown
or chestnut.
Physique light frame,
small straight head, long
back and low-set tail.

Features hardy, active.
Temperament gentle and
easy to handle, but can be
obstinate.
Use light agricultural
work, trotting races, as a
children's pony.

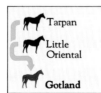

Hackney Horse

Groningen

Warmblood
Origin Groningen, Holland.
Height 15.3 hands.
Colour dark colours.
Physique straight profile, long ears, deep powerful body and high-set tail.
Features frugal with a stylish action.
Temperament gentle, obedient and willing.
Use light draught, riding and driving.

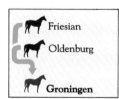

Hackney

Warmblood and Pony
Origin UK.

Height horse, 15.1 hands; pony, under 14.2 hands.
Colour dark colours.
Physique smallish head, strong straightish shoulder, powerful hind quarters and tail set and carried high.
Features high stepping action.
Temperament spirited, alert, vigorous.

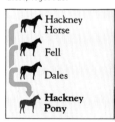

Hanoverian

Halfinger

Pony
Origin The Tirol, Austria.
Height 14 hands.
Colour chestnut with
flaxen mane and tail.
Physique head tapers to
muzzle, broad chest, deep
girth, long, broad back
and short legs.

Features frugal, tough,
sure-footed and long-
lived.
Temperament docile,
good tempered, adaptable
and hard working.
Use mountain pony, riding
driving and pack work.

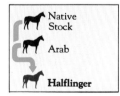

Hanoverian

Warmblood
Origin Hanover and
Lower Saxony, W.
Germany.
Height 16 hands.
Colour solid colours.
Physique powerful.
Features athletic.
Temperament intelligent,

courageous and versatile.
Use competition and
riding horse.

Highland

Hessen, Rheinlander

German Warm Bloods

Arab

Throughbred

Hessian Rheinlander Pfalz

Warmblood
Origin W. Germany.
Height 16 hands.
Physique strongly built.
Features good action.
Temperament good-tempered and adaptable.
Use riding.

Highland

Pony
Origin Western Isles and Scottish mainland.
Height mainland (Garron). 14.2 hands; islands (Western Isles), 13.2 hands.
Colour mainland, black or brown varying to dun and grey; islands, dun with a dorsal stripe, usually with black points and silver mane and tail.
Physique mainland, short ears, powerful loins, strong, short legs with feather tufts and full mane and tail; islands, smaller and finer.
Features strength.
Temperament intelligent, docile, sensitive and responsive.
Use mainland; deer stalking and work for crofters; islands, as children's pony.

Celtic Pony

Galloway

Arab

Highland Western Isles

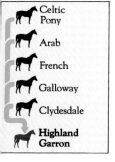

Celtic Pony

Arab

French

Galloway

Clydesdale

Highland Garron

Hispano Anglo-Arab

Warmblood
Origin Estramadura and Andalusia, Spain.
Height 15.3 hands.
Colour bay, chestnut or grey.
Physique Arab features.
Features quick and nimble.
Temperament brave and intelligent.
Use competitions, riding, and testing young bulls.

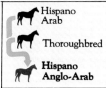

Hispano Arab

Thoroughbred

Hispano Anglo-Arab

Hokaido (Hocaido)

Pony
Origin Japan.
Height 13.1 hands.
Colour black, brown, bay or dun.
Physique like the Mongolian — thickset, short-coupled.
Features tough and strong.
Temperament adaptable and dependable.
Use general work pony.

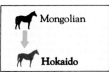

Mongolian

Hokaido

Holstein

Holstein

Warmblood
Origin Emsburg district of
Holstein, W. Germany.
Height 16.1 hands.
Colour black, bay or
brown.
Physique heavy frame
with a strong, muscular
neck and deep girth.

Features good action.
Temperament intelligent,
obedient, good-tempered
and spirited.

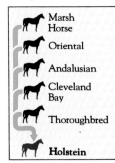

Huzul

Pony
Origin Carpathian
mountains, Poland.
Height 13.2 hands.
Colour dun or bay.
Physique Tarpan head
and robust body.
Features tough and
frugal.

Temperament willing,
good-tempered.
Use pack and agricultural.

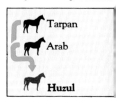

Iceland

Iceland Pony

friendly, but independent.
Use mining, pack and
communication.

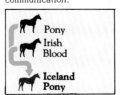

Pony

Origin Iceland.
Height 12.2 hands.
Colour grey, dun.
Physique stocky, compact
body, full mane and tail.
Features tough, able to
amble.
Temperament docile and

Irish Draught

Iomud

Warmblood
Origin Central Asia.
Height 14 hands.
Colour grey, chestnut or bay.
Physique like the Akhal Teké but more compact.
Features great stamina, although not as fast as the Akhal Teké.

Temperament adaptable, courageous and enduring.
Use riding and racing.

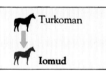

Irish Draught

Coldblood/Warmblood
Origin Ireland.
Height 16 hands.
Colour bay, brown or grey.
Physique straight face, short, muscular neck, longish back, strong, sloping hindquarters, good bone, little feather

and large round feet.
Features good jumper.
Temperament quiet, sensible, willing and active.
Use multi-purpose, but mainly breeding riding horses.

82

Irish Halfbred

Irish Halfbred

Use riding.

Warmblood
Origin Ireland.
Height 16.1 hands.
Colour most colours.
Physique varies.
Features strong and
athletic.
Temperament intelligent,
bold, sensible and
enduring.

Italian Heavy Draught

Italian Heavy Draught

Coldblood
Origin Northern and Central Italy.
Height 15.2 hands.
Colour sorrel or roan.
Physique fine, long head shortish neck, flat back and powerful

hindquarters.
Features fast and strong.
Temperament active, willing, kind and docile.
Use meat and agricultural work.

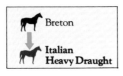

Breton

Italian Heavy Draught

Java

Java

Tarpan

Asiatic
Wild Horse

Java

Pony
Origin Java.
Height 12.2.
Colour most colours.
Physique strong frame.
Features ugly but strong
and tireless.
Temperament willing and
good worker.
Use pulling 'sados' (two-
wheeled taxis).

Jutland

Coldblood
Origin Jutland Island,
Denmark.
Height 15.3 hands.
Colour chestnut or roan.
Physique massive,
compact horse, plain head
and short, feathered legs.
Features easy to handle.

Temperament kind,
gentle.
Use draught.

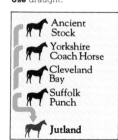

Ancient
Stock

Yorkshire
Coach Horse

Cleveland
Bay

Suffolk
Punch

Jutland

Karabakh

Kabardin

Warmblood
Origin Northern
Caucasus, USSR.
Height 15 hands.
Colour bay or black.
Physique sturdy frame,
short legs and long,
straight back.
Features sure-footed,
tough and long-lived.

Temperament calm,
intelligent and
independent.
Use mountain work as
pack or riding horse, local
equestrian games and
racing.

Mongolian

Turkoman

Arab

Kabardin

Karabair

Warmblood
Origin Uzbekistan, USSR.
Height 15.2 hands.
Colour bay, chestnut, or grey.
Physique similar to the Arab, but stouter. Two types — the Saddle, which is fast and elegant and the Harness, which is larger with a longer back.
Features ancient mountain breed, tough and versatile.
Temperament sensible, brave, intelligent and responsive.
Use agricultural work, riding and local sports.

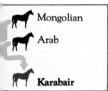

Karabakh

Warmblood
Origin Karabakh mountains, Azerbaidzhan, USSR.
Height 14.2 hands.
Colour dun, bay or chestnut with metallic sheen.
Physique tough mountain horse with a small fine head, low-set tail and good feet.
Features ancient breed, energetic and tough.
Temperament active and sensible.
Use riding, equestrian games and racing.

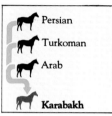

Karacabey

Warmblood
Origin Turkey.
Height 16 hands.
Colour solid colours.
Physique tough.
Features good quality dual-purpose horse.
Temperament reliable.
Use riding, light draught, agricultural work, cavalry and pack.

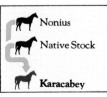

Kathiawari

Pony
Origin Kathiawar province, India.
Height 14.2 hands.
Colour most colours.
Physique light and narrow, with some Arab features.
Features frugal and tough with great stamina.
Temperament uncertain temper, enduring.
Use pack, transport and riding.

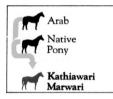

Kazakh

Pony
Origin Kazakh, USSR.
Height 13 hands.
Colour bay, chestnut or grey.
Physique similar to the Mongolian.
Features tough; some ponies amble rather than walk.
Temperament willing and enduring.
Use riding and herding, milk and meat.

Kladruber

Kladruber

Warmblood
Origin Kladruby,
Czechoslovakia.
Height 16.2 hands.
Colour grey.
Physique larger version of
Andalusian.
Features superb carriage
horse.
Temperament proud,
obedient, intelligent and
good tempered.
Use agriculture and
harness.

Knabstrup

Knabstrup

Warmblood
Origin Denmark.
Height 15.3 hands.
Colour spotted, Appaloosa
patterns on roan base.
Physique similar to, but
lighter than, the
Fredericksborg.
Features distinctive
spotted patterning.

Temperament active,
tractable and willing.
Use circus.

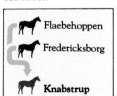

Flaebehoppen
Fredericksborg
Knabstrup

Konik

Konik

Pony
Origin Poland.
Height 13.1 hands.
Colour yellow, grey or
blue dun, usually with
dorsal stripe.
Physique similar to the
Huzul.
Features long-lived,
frugal, hardy; the

foundation stock for many
Polish and Russian breeds.
Temperament
independent, but willing
and good tempered.
Use agricultural work for
lowland farmers.

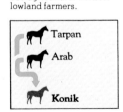

Landais

Pony
Origin the Landes region
of France.
Height 13.2 hands.
Colour dark colours.
Physique varies — usually
fine frame with an Arab-
like head.
Features frugal.
Temperament semi-wild.

Use riding and driving.

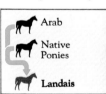

Lipizzaner

Warmblood
Origin Austria.
Height 15.1 hands.
Colour grey.
Physique largish head,

Lipizzaner

small ears, crested neck,
compact body, short,
strong legs and full, fine
mane and tail.
Features athletic, late to
mature.
Temperament excellent
— intelligent, willing and
obedient.
Use high school equitation
and driving.

Arab

Barb

Andalusian

Danish

German

Italian

Lipizzaner

Lithuanian and Latvian

Heavy Draught
Coldblood
Origin Baltic States,
USSR.
Height 15.3 hands.
Colour bay, black or
chestnut with flaxen mane
and tail.
Physique large head,
strong, long neck, sloping
bifurcated croup and little
feather.
Features free, straight
action, strong.
Temperament good
worker, but inclined to be
lazy.
Use draught.

Zemaituka

Oldenburg

Finnish
Draught

Swedish
Ardennes

**Lithuanian
and Latvian**

91

Llanero

Llanero

Warmblood
Origin Venezuela.
Height 14 hands.
Colour dun, yellow with
dark mane and tail, white
and yellow cream or pinto.
Physique lighter frame
than the Criollo; head
similar to Barb.
Features tough.

Temperament courageous
and enduring.
Use ranch work and
transport.

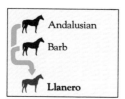

Lokai

Warmblood
Origin Uzbekistan, USSR.
Height 14.3 hands.
Colour grey, bay or
chestnut, often with
golden tint.
Physique varies, but
usually sturdy frame with
tough hooves; hair may be
curly.

Features a strong, sure-
footed mountain horse.
Temperament tractable,
willing and brave.
Use riding, pack, local
equestrian sports.

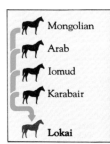

Mangalarga

Lusitana

Warmblood
Origin Southern and
Central Portugal.
Height 15.1 hands.
Colour grey.
Physique small head,
small ears, large eyes,
thick neck, short-coupled,
low-set tail and long legs.
Features frugal, hardy.

Temperament intelligent,
responsive, obedient and
brave.
Use cavalry, and in the
bullring.

Mangalarga

Warmblood
Origin Meiras Gerais,
Brazil.
Height 15 hands.
Colour grey, sorrel, roan
or bay.
Physique longish head,
short back, powerful
hindquarters, low set tail
and long legs.

Features hardy; gait
called 'marcha', between a
canter and a trot.
Temperament intelligent
and enduring, good riding
horse.
Use riding and ranch
work.

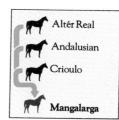

Altér Real
Andalusian
Crioulo
Mangalarga

Manipur

Manipur

Pony
Origin India.
Height 12 hands.
Colour most colours.
Physique thickset with high-set tail.
Features quick and manoeuvrable.
Temperament specialised

polo pony.
Use riding and polo.

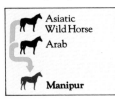

Marwari

Pony.
Origin Marwar province of India.
Height 14.2 hands.
Colour most colours.
Physique light and narrow with some Arab features.
Features frugal and

tough, great stamina.
Temperament tough and enduring, but uncertain temper.
Use pack, transport and riding.

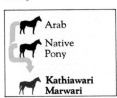

Mecklenburg

Warmblood
Origin E. Germany.
Height 16 hands.
Colour solid colours.

Physique medium head, strong neck, compact body, powerful shoulders and loins.
Features like a slightly smaller Hanoverian.
Temperament willing, bold, kind and tractable.
Use riding, cavalry.

Mongolian Wild Horse

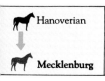

Missouri Foxtrotting

Warmblood
Origin Tennessee, USA.
Height 15.2 hands.
Colour sorrel.
Physique compact, strong body, long neck and intelligent head tapering to muzzle.
Features broken gait called 'foxtrot', walking with forelegs and trotting with hindlegs, at speeds of 10 to 15 mph.
Temperament good temper, enduring, stamina.
Use riding and stock work.

Mongolian Wild Horse

(Asiatic Wild Horse, equus przewalski poliakov).
Pony
Origin Mongolia.
Height 13.1 hands.
Colour black, brown, bay or dun.
Physique thickset, short-coupled, good bone.
Features tough, frugal, great stamina, fast over short distances.
Temperament very enduring, brave.
Use work pony of nomadic tribes; mares provide milk for cheese and a drink called *kumiss*.

95

Morgan

Morgan

Warmblood
Origin Massachusetts, USA.
Height 15 hands.
Colour bay, brown, black, or chestnut.
Physique short, broad head, thick neck, strong shoulders, back and hind quarters, good bone and full mane and tail.
Features versatile, tough high action.
Temperament kind, independent, active and hard working.
Use riding and driving.

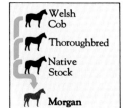

Welsh Cob

Thoroughbred

Native Stock

Morgan

Murakosi

Murakosi .

Coldblood.
Origin Hungary.
Height 16 hands.
Colour chestnut, with
flaxen mane and tail.
Physique strong frame,
little wither, dip in back,
round hindquarters and
little feather.

Features strong and
active.
Temperament docile and
willing.
Use general draught and
agricultural work.

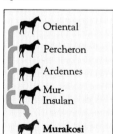

Oriental

Percheron

Ardennes

Mur-
Insulan

Murakosi

Murghese

Warmblood.
Origin Italy.
Height 15.2 hands.
Physique Oriental
features but heavier frame.
Features versatile.
Temperament high-
quality, good tempered.
Use dual-purpose horse
for agricultural work or
riding.

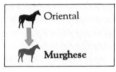

Mustang

Warmblood
Origin western states of
America and Mexico.
Height 14.2 hands.
Colour most colours.
Physique sturdy, tough
lightweight frame, good
bone and tough feet.
Features hardy and
frugal.
Temperament brave and
independent, can be
stubborn.
Use riding, showing, trail
riding, endurance trials,
competitions and stock
work.

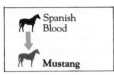

Native Tibetan
(Nanfan)

Pony
Origin Tibet.
Height 12.2. hands.
Colour all colours.
Physique sturdy frame.
Features energetic and
tough.
Temperament intelligent,
active and courageous.
Use riding and general
work.

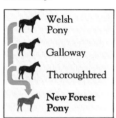

New Forest

Pony
Origin New Forest,
Hampshire, UK.
Height 12-14.2 hands.
Colour solid colours.
Physique great variety —
type A, lighter, under 13.2
hands; type B, heavier,
between 13.2 and 14.2

hands.
Features hardy, frugal.
Temperament brave,
intelligent and willing.
Very friendly and quick to
learn, makes a safe and
ideal children's pony.
Use riding.

Nonius

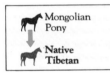

Warmblood
Origin Hungary.
Height large Nonius, over
15.3 hands; small Nonius,
under 15.3 hands.
Physique elegant head,
long neck, strong back.
Features versatile, long-
lived and active.
Temperament willing,

consistent, calm, kind.
Use riding and
agricultural work.

Noriker (South
German
Coldblood)

Coldblood
Origin Austria and
Germany.
Height 16.1 hands.
Colour chestnut, bay,
sometimes spotted.
Physique largish head,
short, thick neck, straight
shoulder, broad back and
short legs with little
feather.
Features sure-footed with
a good action.
Temperament reliable.
Use agricultural and
mountain work.

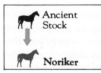

Novokirghiz

Warmblood.
Origin Kirghiz and
Kazakhstan, USSR.
Height 15 hands.
Colour bay, chestnut or
grey.

Oldenburg

Physique long neck, long straight back, sloping croup, short legs.
Features tough, sure-footed and frugal.
Temperament strong and enduring.
Use mountain work — harness and saddle; provides milk.

Kirghiz

Don

Thoroughbred

Novokirghiz

Oldenburg

Warmblood
Origin Oldenburg and East Friesland, W. Germany.
Height 16.3 hands.
Physique largest of the German warmbloods, plain straight head, strong shoulder, deep girth, relatively short legs.

Features matures early.
Temperament bold, kind, sensible.
Use riding and driving.

Andalusian

Barb

Hanoverian

Cleveland Bay

Thoroughbred

Anglo-Norman

Oldenburg

Orlov Trotter

Orlov Trotter

Warmblood
Origin USSR.
Height 16 hands.
Colour grey, black or bay.
Physique thickset, upright
shoulder, broad chest,
deep girth and long
straight back.
Features active and fast.
Temperament bold and

courageous.
Use trotting races, riding,
harness.

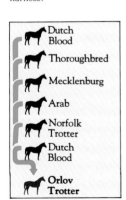

Pahlavan

Warmblood
Origin Iran.
Height 15.2-16 hands.
Colour solid colours.
Physique strong and
elegant.
Features developed by
crossing Plateau Persian
with Arab and
Thoroughbred.

Temperament spirited.
Use riding.

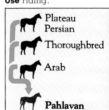

100

Palomino

Palomino

Warmblood
Origin California, USA.
Height 14 hands.
Colour golden with no
markings other than white
on face or below the knees;
mane and tail white, silver,
or ivory; dark eyes.
Physique varies;
registered for colour, so

does not yet breed true to
type.
Features distinctive
colouration.
Temperament intelligent,
good general-purpose
horse.
Use riding, driving and
stock work.

Paso Fino

Warmblood
Origin Puerto Rico.
Height 14.3 hands.
Colour most colours.
Physique Arab-like head,
strong back, loins and
quarters and hard legs,
which are light of bone.
Features spirited; extra
four-beat gaits, of which

the slowest is the *paso fino*,
then the *paso corto* and the
paso largo.
Temperament alert,
tractable and willing.
Use riding.

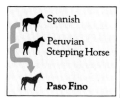

Spanish

Peruvian
Stepping Horse

Paso Fino

Percheron

Peneia

Pony
Origin Peneia,
Peloponnese, Greece.
Height 10-14 hands.
Colour most colours.
Physique Oriental.
Features frugal and
hardy.
Temperament willing.

Use pack and agricultural
work.

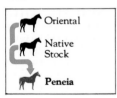

Percheron

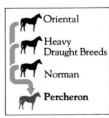

Coldblood.
Origin France.
Height 16.1 hands.
Colour grey or black.
Physique Oriental-type
head, strong, well-
proportioned body, full
mane and tail, clean, hard
legs without feather.
Features good action and

great presence.
Temperament energetic,
intelligent and docile.
Use draught.

Persian Arab

Persian Arab.

Temperament spirited
and intelligent.
Use riding, and improving
other breeds.

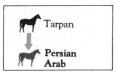

Tarpan

Persian
Arab

Thoroughbred.
Origin Iran.
Height 15 hands.
Colour grey or bay.
Physique elegant,
compact body, otherwise
as Arab.
Features possibly older
than the desert Arab.

Peruvian Stepping Horse

Peruvian Stepping Horse

special extended gait,
similar to an amble.
Temperament enduring,
thrives under stress.
Use riding and stock work.

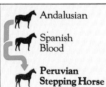

Warmblood
Origin Peru.
Height 15 hands.
Colour bay or chestnut.
Physique broad chest,
short-coupled, and strong
round hindquarters.
Features endurance and a

Pindos

Pony
Origin mountains of
Thessaly and Epirus,
Greece.
Height 12.1 hands.
Colour grey or dark
colours.
Physique tough, light
frame.
Features mountain pony,

mares often used to breed
mules.
Temperament hardy.
Use riding and light
agricultural work.

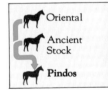

Pinto

Pinto

Warmblood
Origin USA.
Height varies.
Colour black with white or white with any colour but black.
Physique varies.
Features colour breed, traditionally associated with American Indians.

Temperament intelligent and enduring.
Use ranch work riding, showing.

Plateau Persian

Warmblood
Origin Central Persian Plateau.
Height 15 hands.
Colour grey, bay or chestnut.
Physique Arab features, but this varies as it is an amalgamation of separate breeds.
Features good action, strong and sure-footed.
Temperament has fire and character.
Use riding.

Arab
Shiragazi
Quashquai
Darashouri
Basseri
Bahhtiari
Jaf
Plateau Persian

Pleven

Warmblood
Origin Bulgaria.
Height 15.2 hands.
Colour chestnut.
Physique sturdier version. of the Arab.
Features robust.
Temperament kind, brave, intelligent and spirited.
Use all-purpose.

Local Arab
Hungarian Gidran Arab
Strelets Anglo-Arab
Gidran Anglo-Arab
Local Anglo Arab
Pleven

Poitevin

Coldblood
Origin Poitiers, France.
Height 16.3 hands.
Colour dun.
Physique plain conformation, large head, long body, big feet with heavy feather.
Features docile.
Temperament relatively unintelligent and can be lethargic.
Use mares put to Baudet Poitevins (jackasses of about 16 hands), to breed large mules.

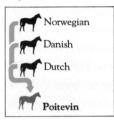

Norwegian
Danish
Dutch
Poitevin

Polish Arab

Warmblood
Origin Poland.
Height 14.3 hands.
Colour grey, chestnut or bay.
Physique similar to the Arab, but with more sloping quarters and tail carried lower.
Temperament like Arab, bold, spirited, intelligent.
Use racing, breeding and riding.

Pony of the Americas

Pony
Origin USA.
Height 12.1 hands.
Colour Appaloosa. patterns.
Physique Arab-like head, short back and round body.
Features smooth, free action.
Temperament willing, gentle and versatile, ideal as children's pony.

Shetland Pony
Appaloosa
Pony of the Americas

Quarter Horse

Quarter-Horse

Warmblood
Origin USA.
Height 15.3 hands.
Colour solid colours, usually chestnut.
Physique short head, powerful, short-coupled body, large round hindquarters and fine legs.
Features fast and

versatile.
Temperament intelligent, sensible, active and nimble.
Use riding, racing, ranch work and rodeos.

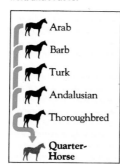

Arab

Barb

Turk

Andalusian

Thoroughbred

Quarter-Horse

Rhineland Heavy Draught
(Rhenish-German)

Coldblood
Origin W. Germany.
Height 16.1 hands.
Colour chestnut or chestnut roan with flaxen mane and tail.
Physique heavy and

compact with short, feathered legs.
Features strength, early maturity.
Temperament obliging, mature and good-tempered.
Use draught.

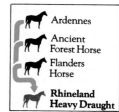

Ardennes

Ancient
Forest Horse

Flanders
Horse

**Rhineland
Heavy Draught**

Saddlebred

Russian Heavy Draught

Coldblood
Origin Ukraine, USSR.
Height 14.2 hands.
Colour chestnut, bay or roan.
Physique the smallest coldblood; thickset, massive neck, broad back

and sloping croup.
Features strong active and fast.
Temperament good-tempered and lively.
Use agricultural work.

Swedish Ardennes
Percheron
Orlov Trotter
Indigenous Ukraine stock
Russian Heavy Draught

Russian Trotter

Warmblood.
Origin USSR.
Height 15.3 hands.
Colour black, bay or chestnut.
Physique mixture of Orlov and Standard-bred characteristics.
Features faster than the Orlov.
Temperament like the

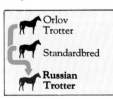

Orlov Trotter
Standardbred
Russian Trotter

Orlov — active, bold and courageous.
Use trotting races.

Saddlebred

Warmblood
Origin USA.
Height 15.2 hands.
Colour black, brown, bay, grey or chestnut.
Physique small head with

Salerno

traight profile. Strong
>ody and hindquarters,
ail carried artificially
iigh.
'eatures five gaited
iction, three normal gaits
>lus a four-beat rack, at
vhich it can reach 30
nph.
'emperament great
>resence, gentle and

sweet temper.
Use showing, riding and
driving.

Salerno

Warmblood
Origin Meremma and
Salerno, Italy.
Height 16 hands.
Colour solid colours.
Physique large, refined
head and good
conformation.
Features aristocratic,

quality saddle horse.
Temperament intelligent
responsive and gentle.
Use riding, especially
army.

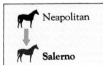

Schleswig Heavy Draught

Sandalwood

Pony
Origin Indonesia.
Height 13 hands.
Colour dun with dorsal stripe, dark mane and tail.
Physique lighter frame, finer coat and more elegant than other Indonesian ponies.

Features fast.
Temperament hard-working and enduring.
Use bareback racing and general work.

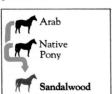

Arab

Native Pony

Sandalwood

Schleswig Heavy Draught

Coldblood.
Origin W. Germany.
Height 15.2-16 hands.
Colour chestnut, flaxen mane and tail.
Physique similar to the Jutland — plain, close-coupled, little feather.

Features active, good mover.
Temperament kind, gentle and willing.
Use draught.

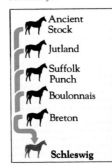

Ancient Stock

Jutland

Suffolk Punch

Boulonnais

Breton

Schleswig

Shagya Arab

Selle Francais

Features athletic.
Temperament brave,
calm and good-tempered.
Use riding and
competitions.

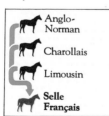

Warmblood
Origin Northern France.
Height 16 hands.
Colour solid colours.
Physique robust frame,
powerful shoulder, strong
longish back, deep girth
and powerful
hindquarters.

Shagya Arab

Warmblood
Origin Hungary.
Height 15 hands.
Colour grey.
Physique Arab features.
small head.
Features hardy, frugal
and active.
Temperament versatile,

alert and intelligent.
Use cavalry, general
riding and driving.

111

Shetland

Shetland

Pony
Origin Shetland and
Orkney Islands, UK.
Height 9.3 hands (6.2
hands the smallest yet
recorded).
Colour black, brown or
coloured.
Physique small head, face

usually concave, small
ears, short, strong back,
full mane and tail; winter
coat very thick, summer
coat fine and sleek.
Features hardy and
strong; can pull loads
twice its own weight.
Temperament very gentle
and courageous, easy to
train.
Use mining, general work,
driving and riding.

Celtic
Pony

Shetland
Pony

Shire

Shire

Coldblood
Origin central counties, UK.
Height 17 hands.
Colour dark with white markings.
Physique face nearly convex, broad forehead, long, crested neck, broad back, sloping croup and much fine silky feather.
Features strength; the tallest breed in the world.
Temperament docile and gentle, active, industrious and adaptable.
Use pack, agricultural work and riding.

Old English
Black Horse

Flanders
Horse

Native
Stock

Shire

Skyros

Skyros

Pony
Origin Island of Skyros,
Greece.
Height 10 hands.
Colour dun, brown or
grey.
Physique light bone,
upright shoulder, often
cow-hocked.

Features an ancient
breed; Greece's smallest
pony.
Temperament tough work
pony.
Use pack, carrying water,
agricultural work and
riding.

Sokolsky

Warmblood
Origin Poland.
Height 15.2 hands.
Colour chestnut, brown or
grey.
Physique large head,
sturdy frame, short,
straight back, short legs
and large round feet with

little feather.
Features frugal.
Temperament kind, calm,
patient and hard-working.
Use agricultural work.

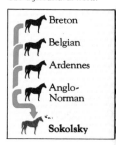

Standardbred

Sorraia

Pony
Origin River Sorraia district, Portugal.
Height 13 hands.
Colour dun, with a dorsal stripe and stripes on legs.
Physique primitive appearance, long head, straight profile, long ears, thin neck and straight

back.
Features tough and frugal.
Temperament enduring.
Use runs wild.

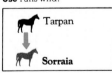

Spiti

Pony
Origin India.
Height 12 hands.
Colour grey.
Physique thickset and short-coupled.
Features sure-footed and tough.
Temperament intelligent,

alert and tireless, but not always good-tempered.
Use transportation in mountains.

Standardbred

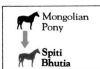

Warmblood
Origin USA.
Height 15.2 hands.
Colour solid colours.
Physique varies as it is bred for speed; usually muscular Thoroughbred type with longer back, short legs and powerful

115

Suffolk Punch

shoulders.
Features stamina, speed.

Thoroughbred

Canadian Trotter

Hackney

Narrangansett Pacer

Arab

Barb

Morgan

Standardbred

Temperament bold, active, brave and enduring.
Use driving and racing.

Suffolk Punch

Coldblood
Origin east Anglia, UK.
Height 16.1 hands.
Colour chestnut, with no white markings.
Physique short clean legs, massive neck and shoulders, square body.
Features good action, frugal and long-lived.

Temperament kind, active and intelligent.
Use draught.

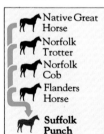

Native Great Horse

Norfolk Trotter

Norfolk Cob

Flanders Horse

Suffolk Punch

Sumba

Use dancing and general work.

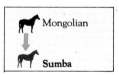

Mongolian

Sumba

ny
igin Indonesia.
ight 12.2 hands.
lour dun with dorsal
ipe, dark mane and tail.
ysique primitive type.
atures special use as a
ncing pony.
mperament tough,
lling and intelligent.

Swedish Halfbred

Swedish Ardennes

Coldblood
Origin Sweden.
Height 15.3 hands.
Colour black, brown, bay or chestnut.
Physique similar to, but smaller than, the Belgian Ardennes.
Features active.

Temperament energetic, quiet and kindly.
Use agricultural work and timber hauling.

Swedish Halfbred

Warmblood
Origin Sweden.
Height 16.1 hands.
Colour any solid colour.
Physique smallish, intelligent head, large bold eye, longish neck, deep girth and straightish back.
Features extravagant, straight action.
Temperament intelligent, bold, sensible and obedient.
Use general riding and competitions.

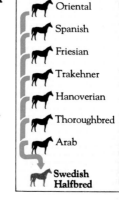

Tarpan

Swiss Halfbred

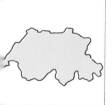

Warmblood
Origin Switzerland.
Height 16.1 hands.
Colour any solid colour.
Physique well-made,
strong horse.
Features athletic, with a
good action.
Temperament good-

tempered and versatile.
Use riding and driving.

Thoroughbred
Anglo-Norman
Holstein
Trakehner
Hanoverian
Swedish Halfbred
Swiss Halfbred

Tarpan (equus przevalskii gmellini antonius)

Pony
Origin Poland.
Height 13 hands.
Colour brown or dun with
dorsal stripe, dark mane
and tail, and stripes on

forelegs and inner thighs;
coat may change to white
in winter.
Physique long head,
longish ears, short neck
longish back and fine legs.
Features tough and
fertile.
Temperament
independent, brave and
tenacious.
Use exhibited in zoos and
also roams wild.

Equus Celticus

Tarpan

Tennessee Walking Horse

Tennessee Walking Horse

Warmblood
Origin Tennessee, USA.
Height 15.2 hands.
Colour solid colours.
Physique common head, crested neck, strong, sloping shoulder, powerful loins and hindquarters, clean legs and full mane and tail, carried artificially high.
Features running walk, with the forefeet raised high and the hind legs moving with long strides.

Temperament docile, kind willing and alert.
Use showing and riding.

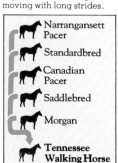

Narrangansett Pacer

Standardbred

Canadian Pacer

Saddlebred

Morgan

Tennessee Walking Horse

120

Tersky

Tersky

Warmblood
Origin Stavropol region,
USSR.
Height 15 hands.
Colour grey.
Physique Arab features.
Features three types,
light, medium and
thickset.
Temperament kind,

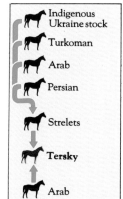

Indigenous
Ukraine stock

Turkoman

Arab

Persian

Strelets

Tersky

Arab

intelligent and enduring.
Use racing, competitions
and the circus.

Thoroughbred

Thoroughbred

Thoroughbred
Origin UK.
Height 16 hands.
Colour solid colours.
Physique varies from close-coupled sprinters with large, powerful hindquarters to big-framed, longer backed,

big-boned chasers. Must have an elegant head, long neck, sloping shoulder, prominent wither and silky coat.
Features fast and active.
Temperament bold, brave and spirited.

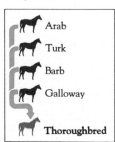

Arab

Turk

Barb

Galloway

Thoroughbred

Use racing, riding and improving other breeds.

Timor

Pony
Origin Timor, Indonesia.
Height 11.1 hands.
Colour dark colours.
Physique fine but sturdy frame.

Features agile.
Temperament possesses common sense, willingness and endurance.
Use agricultural work and transportation.

Tarpan

Asiatic
Wild Horse

Timor

Toric

Warmblood
Origin Estonia, USSR.

Trakehner

Height 15.1 hands.
Colour chestnut or bay.
Physique long, muscular body, short strong legs with light feather.
Features great strength and stamina.
Temperament good-tempered, calm and hard working.
Use light draught.

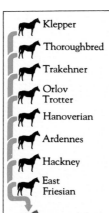

Klepper
Thoroughbred
Trakehner
Orlov Trotter
Hanoverian
Ardennes
Hackney
East Friesian
Toric

Trakehner (East Prussian)

Warmblood
Origin East Prussia.
Height 16.1 hands.
Colour dark colours.
Physique head is broad between the eyes, tapering to the muzzle; long

straight neck, prominent withers, deep girth and flattish hind quarters.
Features extravagant action.
Temperament intelligent, active, good-tempered and loyal.
Use competitions and riding.

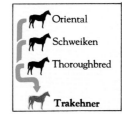

Oriental
Schweiken
Thoroughbred
Trakehner

Vladimir Heavy Draught

Turkoman
(Turkmen)

Warmblood
Origin Iran.
Height 15.2 hands.
Colour solid colours.
Physique narrow chest,
light but tough frame.
Features floating action

and speed.
Temperament enduring.
Use foundation stock for
other breeds, riding,
cavalry and racing.

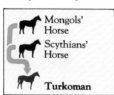

Mongols'
Horse

Scythians'
Horse

Turkoman

Viatka

Pony
Origin Viatsky territory —
Baltic States, USSR.
Height 13.2 hands.
Colour dark, sometimes
with dorsal stripe.
Physique plain head,
sturdy frame, broad,
straight back, short legs

with good bone.
Features frugal, tough
and fast.
Temperament obedient.
Use all-purpose pony.

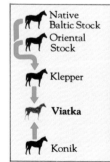

Native
Baltic Stock

Oriental
Stock

Klepper

Viatka

Konik

Vladimir Heavy Draught

Coldblood
Origin Vladimir district, SSR.
Height 16 hands.
Colour any solid colour.
Physique strong frame, good conformation, with feather on legs.
Features active and powerful.
Temperament energetic, competitive and hard-working.
Use draught.

- Cleveland Bay
- Suffolk Punch
- Shire
- Ardennes
- Percheron
- **Vladimir Heavy Draught**

Welsh Cob
(Section D)

Warmblood
Origin Wales, UK.
Height 14-15.1 hands.
Colour solid colours.
Physique compact, great substance, quality head, strong shoulder, deep, powerful back and silky feather.
Features strength, stamina; high knee action.
Temperament bold, equable intelligent and energetic.
Use all purpose; driving and riding.

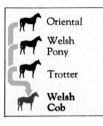

- Oriental
- Welsh Pony
- Trotter
- Welsh Cob

Welsh Mountain
(Section A)

Pony
Origin Wales, UK.
Height under 12 hands.
Colour grey, brown or chestnut.
Physique Arab-like head, long, crested neck, sloping shoulder, short back and high set tail.
Features great endurance.
Temperament intelligent, high-spirited and courageous.
Use riding, foundation stock for children's riding ponies.

Welsh Pony
(Section B)

Pony
Origin Wales, UK.
Height 12-13.2 hands.
Colour solid colours.
Physique larger version of Section A.
Features good action.
Temperament intelligent, high-spirited, kind, good children's pony.
Use riding.

- Welsh Mountain Pony
- Welsh Cob
- Thoroughbred
- Welsh Pony

Welsh Pony

Welsh Pony
(Section C)

Pony
Origin Wales, UK.
Height under 13.2 hands.
Colour solid colours.
Physique cob type, with silky feather.
Features hardy, active and frugal.

Temperament stout-hearted.
Use driving and trekking.

Westphalian

Warmblood
Origin Westphalia, W. Germany.
Height 16.1 hands.
Colour any solid colour.

Physique similar to the Hanoverian.
Features developed from the Hanoverian — good general-purpose horse.
Temperament courageous, intelligent and versatile.
Use riding, competitions and driving.

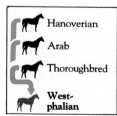

Hanoverian
Arab
Thoroughbred
West-phalian

Wielkopolski

Warmblood
Origin Poland.
Height 16 hands.
Colour chestnut or bay.
Physique a compact, well proportioned horse.
Features formed by amalgamating the Masuren and Posnan.

Wielkopolski

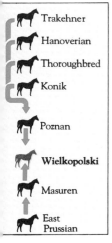

Trakehner

Hanoverian

Thoroughbred

Konik

Poznan

Wielkopolski

Masuren

East
Prussian

Temperament excellent, courageous and hard-working.
Use riding competitions and light draught.

Württemburg

Warmblood
Origin Württemburg, W. Germany.

Height 16 hands.
Colour black, brown, bay or chestnut.
Physique cob type —

Arab

Anglo-Norman

Nonius

Oldenburg

Trakehner

Suffolk
Punch

Württemburg

straight profile to face, deep girth, straight back and good bone.
Features hardy, with great stamina.
Temperament gentle, hard-working and willing.
Use riding and driving.

Zemaituka
(Pechora)

Pony
Origin Baltic States, USSR.
Height 13.2 hands.
Colour brown, palomino or dun with dorsal stripe.
Physique straight face, smallish ears, short neck

and straight back.
Features hardy and frugal.
Temperament good-tempered intelligent, willing and energetic.
Use riding and work.

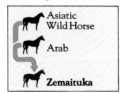

Asiatic Wild Horse

Arab

Zemaituka